D0462144

"Hey, Father!"

"Hey, Father!"

32 Stories From a Doorman in the House of God

FR. GORDON DOUGLAS

CHARIS

SERVANT PUBLICATIONS
ANN ARBOR, MICHIGAN

Copyright 2001 by Fr. Gordon Douglas
All rights reserved.

Charis Books is an imprint of Servant Publications especially designed to serve
Roman Catholics.

Scripture texts used in this work are taken from the New American Bible. The
Old Testament of the New American Bible © 1970 by the Confraternity of
Christian Doctrine (CCD), Washington, D.C. (Books 1 Samuel to 2 Macaccabees
© 1969 1986 CCD; Revised Psalms of the New American Bible © 1991 CCD.)
All rights reserved.

Most of the stories in this book have been used with permission. Otherwise,
names and identifying details have been changed to provide anonymity.

Published by Servant Publications
P.O. Box 8617
Ann Arbor, Michigan 48107

Cover design by Paul Higdon, Minneapolis, Minn.

01 02 03 04 10 9 8 7 6 5 4 3 2 1

Printed in the United States of America
ISBN 1-56955-237-1

LIBRARY OF CONGRESS CATALOGING-IN-PUBLICATION DATA

Douglas, Gordon, 1942-
    Hey, Father! : 32 stories from a doorman in the house of God /
Gordon Douglas.
        p. cm.
    Includes bibliographical references.
    ISBN 1-56955-237-1 (alk. paper)
    1. School chaplains—Religious life—Anecdotes 2. Catholic
Church—Clergy—Biography. I. Title.
    BV4376 .D68 2001
    282'.092—dc21

                                                    2001003665

Contents

Introduction

I'm a Catholic priest. That's all I've ever wanted to be.

I suspect that when the good Lord placed me in my mother's womb, he equipped me with a "priest gene." Most kids go through dozens of career dreams as they grow up, but not me. I never wavered. From my earliest days, I was drawn to the magical and mysterious world of the Catholic Church. I wanted to be in the center of that wondrous world, and I figured the priesthood was as close to the center as I could possibly get— at least this side of heaven. When my friends were outside playing cops and robbers, I was inside playing priest. I preached to my dog, made "communion" wafers by compressing bits of sandwich bread, and wore a vestment I fashioned from my blankie.

If God didn't put the priest gene in me, my family did. I grew up in a very, very Catholic family whose love and passion for the Catholic Church was unmistakable. The spiritual, social, and educational center of our family life was our parish church and school, St. Margaret's. It was a modest slice of Catholic life, to be sure, but for me St. Margaret's held all the wonder of St. Peter's Basilica in Rome. The parish priests and nuns frequently visited our home, often staying for dinner. Until I watched them eat, I hadn't thought priests and nuns had bodily needs. The revelation stunned me.

"Father" always knew best, and my parents consulted him

whenever they had to make a serious decision. They always sided with the nuns at school; my version of the story never had a prayer. As a family, we rarely missed daily Mass and Saturday night confession, we said the family rosary after every evening meal, and we always made sure we were home to watch Archbishop Sheen's popular television show of the 1950s, *Life Is Worth Living.*

The first Catholic priest to come into my life was Fr. Philip Corboy, the pastor of St. Margaret's who baptized me. Later he was elevated to Monsignor Corboy and got to wear purple piping on his black robes. That purple piping made him even more special in my eyes. My parents respected him and quoted him more often than they quoted President Truman. I don't know if I feared this priest with the purple piping on his black robe, but I was certainly in awe of him. Fr. Corboy was larger than life to a young boy like me.

One Christmas when I was about four, Fr. Corboy stopped by our home to pay a pastoral visit—coming on a day like Christmas, an honor that ranked up there with the Virgin Mary's visit to her cousin, Elizabeth. The fact that my father was the number-one contributor to the parish might have prompted his appearance at our door. Whatever the reason, we rolled out the red carpet, and our greeting would have out-done the pomp and pageantry of "Hail to the Chief."

When Fr. Corboy had made himself comfortable in my father's favorite chair (it was off-limits to the rest of us), I eagerly waited for my parent's gushing to subside so I could ask Fr. Corboy a question that had been on my mind for some time: did he have any kids? When the conversation finally hit a lull, I saw my chance and blurted out, "Hey, Father!"

Introduction

I got no further. My mother and father, looking pained and embarrassed, sent me to my room before I could get another word out. I was stunned. What had I done? Even a belch at the dinner table had never resulted in a trip to my room!

Time dragged by. Finally I heard my parents see Fr. Corboy to the door. A moment later they entered my room, disappointment on their faces, and I learned the reason for my banishment.

"You say 'hey' to a dog or your playmates," my father sternly lectured me. "*Never* address a priest as 'Hey, Father!'" Then in his best Catholic language, he explained that a priest is an *altus Christus*, a member of God's nobility. "Addressing a priest as 'Hey, Father' drags him down to your level," he told me. "You should have said, 'Excuse me, Father, I have a question for you.'"

Thank God my dad didn't know the question I'd planned to ask, or I'm sure he would have put me up for adoption. I'd brought enough disgrace on our family as it was.

Of course I had meant no disrespect to Fr. Corboy. My approach was simply a curious child's way of knocking on the door of his life, which I saw as the door to the Catholic world that so entranced me: a world of saints and sinners, heaven and hell, pope and bishops, nuns and priests, incense and candles, pews and pulpits, hymns and chants, confessionals and altars, stained-glass windows and marble statues, rosaries and holy cards, St. Christopher medals and prayer books, May processions and first Holy Communions. I wanted admission into that Catholic world; instead, I was sent to my room.

I know that if my well-intentioned parents hadn't intervened, Fr. Corboy would have warmly and widely opened the doors of his life to me. I know because in the following years at St. Margaret's and at other Catholic schools and parishes, I knocked often and was always granted entrance by priests like Fr. Philip Corboy. Like a PIN number to the Christian faith, the words "Hey, Father!" gave me access to the world I longed to know.

The title of this book springs in part from my vivid memory of that Christmas visit from Fr. Corboy. But I have an even more compelling reason for having chosen "Hey, Father!" as my title. In the last thirty-three years, not a day has gone by that I haven't heard somebody say those words to me. When I hear them, I do my best to listen—and to grant the person who utters them entrance into my life and world.

I was ordained a Catholic priest of the archdiocese of Seattle on May 18, 1968. The archbishop looked over my seminary records and immediately sent me out of town, to a rural parish as far away from Seattle as one could get. My dreams of being a monsignor and wearing purple piping went out the window. But I liked the parish, and I liked being a priest.

Three years later, the phone rang. It was the archbishop, calling to tell me he was transferring me to Bishop Blanchet High School in Seattle, where I would be a faculty member and the school chaplain.

I can't say I was pleased with the assignment. I thought that "real Christian ministry" meant being the pastor of a parish, not teacher and chaplain to fourteen hundred longhaired teenagers who were protesting everything from being sent to a Catholic school to the Vietnam War. But in the 1970s, when an archbishop said "Go!" to one of his priests, you went. (There's a bit more wiggle room today.) So I went, with the understanding it was a three-year assignment, after which I'd return to my "real priest work."

That was thirty years ago. I'm still the chaplain at Bishop Blanchet High School in Seattle, and I wouldn't have it any other way.

It's not a predictable job. I'm constantly surprised at what each new day brings me. In fact, the only thing I know with certainty is that every day I'll hear the words "Hey, Father!" I might hear them at a cemetery, in a hallway outside a courtroom, or on the sidelines during a junior varsity football game. They might come from a troubled bridesmaid at a wedding reception, a young couple leaving church on Sunday morning, or a teary-eyed teenage girl who has come to my office between classes. Whenever I hear them, I know a story will follow.

This book is about those stories: stories about people who are struggling to make sense out of their lives, people who want to find meaning for their lives. They come to me hoping the Christian faith will offer them that meaning. They knock on the door of my life, just as I once knocked on the door of Fr. Corboy's life, because I wear a Roman collar. Sometimes they turn away, disappointed; sometimes they find what they are seeking.

I hope you enjoy the stories in this book. Even more, I hope they will bolster your Christian faith, that reading about what God has done in the lives of others will help you make sense of what he is doing in your own life as well.

SECTION ONE

"Hey, Father!
What Does God Want From Me?"

CHAPTER ONE

It All Starts With Attitude

One day, a number of years ago, the high school principal hauled me into his office and said, "Father, the freshmen need a wrestling coach. You're it."

Mind you, I knew nothing about wrestling. The closest I had ever come to a wrestling match was rolling around on the floor with my older brother. I had certainly never been on a wrestling team. But turning a deaf ear to my protestations, the principal handed me an illustrated book on wrestling and said, "Practice starts on Monday."

On my first day on the job, I gathered the team around me. Their curiosity about the new coach quickly changed to alarm as I pointed to the photographs in the book and said, "This is what I want you to do." We didn't win a single meet that year and very few in the years that followed, but we did learn a lot of things that were not in that book.

During my second year as a wrestling coach, our team had an away meet with a powerhouse team. When we walked into the locker room, the opposing coach came up to me and said, "Father, I have a favor to ask. I have a senior heavyweight who doesn't get a lot of mat time on varsity. Can your freshman heavyweight wrestle him today?"

I looked at him curiously. The age and experience difference made it an obvious mismatch, and he knew it. As I opened my mouth to say no, he added, "Before you make up your mind, I want you to meet the young man."

"Hey, Father!"

As we strolled over to the other team's locker room, he told me the senior heavyweight had cerebral palsy. His left arm and leg were, for all practical purposes, nonfunctional. But despite his disability, the young man had been wrestling competitively since junior high school. He had been elected captain of the team four out of six years and been named "Most Inspirational" six out of six years. He had never missed a practice. He never left early. He never used his cerebral palsy as an excuse. He had competed in seventy-four matches and had lost all seventy-four—all of them by being pinned, which even I knew is the most humbling way to lose a wrestling match.

When I heard this young man's story and then met him, I knew that God had something special in mind. I went back to Mark, our freshman heavyweight, and filled him in.

"Do you want to take him on, Mark? It's up to you," I told him.

Mark, who possessed a heart every bit as big as his 210-pound body, said, "If it's all right with you, Father, then it's OK with me." He hadn't been around long enough to question my judgment.

As the time drew near for their match, I sensed that Mark didn't want to be the seventy-fifth wrestler to beat the courageous senior. "Should I let him win?" he asked me. His question hung in the air for a minute, and then he answered it himself: "That would be even worse for him, wouldn't it?" He went out to the mat and less than a minute into the first period pinned his opponent with ease.

After the match, I approached the senior wrestler, and with my foot firmly and deeply planted in my mouth said, "Son, I think it's wonderful, with your disability, that you're out here competing." The boy looked hurt. "Hey, Father, what disability?"

he asked. Suddenly, I felt very small and very stupid.

So often, many of us associate the word "disability" with images of wheelchairs, crutches, special lifts on buses, and reserved parking spaces. But as this young wrestler was quick to point out, a physical limitation doesn't have to limit our ability to contribute fully. This young man may have had cerebral palsy, but he didn't withdraw from life. He participated fully with the gifts he had. What he didn't score in points on the board, he made up in leadership and inspiration. His attitude taught me that the only true disability a person can have is failing to make the most out of what God gives him.

The world celebrates the heroism of Mother Teresa, a small woman with a big heart. She wasn't physically strong, but she didn't let that get in her way—she didn't need great strength to bathe a leper, hold the hand of the dying, or feed the hungry. Mother Teresa has been called one of the world's greatest people. She is universally proclaimed a saint, not because of her physical abilities but because of her spirit of love, compassion, and service.

She was Christ to everyone she met.

One of the most powerful scenes in the Gospel of Luke describes the time a paralyzed man was brought to Jesus for healing. Do you remember what Jesus said to him? Not "Rise and walk!" but "Son, your sins are forgiven."

That wasn't what the man had come to hear. He wanted to walk, to dance, to go fishing with his friends, to get married, and have children. He didn't want forgiveness of sins! But Jesus knew what the man himself didn't know. Jesus knew that what he needed more than physical restoration was spiritual healing.

Our attitude about life comes out of our spirit. Out of a diseased spirit springs a diseased attitude; out of a healthy spirit springs a healthy attitude. The senior heavyweight in the story I just told had a healthy attitude. So did Mark.

As for me—I'm working on it. I hope you are, too.

CHAPTER TWO

A Giant for God

We Catholics get a bad rap when it comes to the saints of our Christian history. Our use and love of statues, medals, and images of the saints puzzles and even confounds those Christians who think our shared faith should center only on Christ.

I have to admit their concern has some legitimacy. I, too, get concerned when I hear stories about people who dig a hole in their front yard, stick a statue of St. Joseph upside down in it, and bury the poor man alive, believing this will hasten the sale of their house. Stories of statues that weep or bleed leave me scratching my head. But a few people going to extremes doesn't negate the help and inspiration we can receive from the stories of the saints.

St. Christopher has always been my favorite saint. In the 1980s when the Catholic Church dropped him from the official list of the saints, I went into a depression. Almost daily people asked me and other priests if St. Chris was still a saint. The question wasn't exactly on a par with abortion, birth control, euthanasia, and other smoldering moral issues, but its frequency said something about the importance of this saint for many Catholics, myself included.

The declaration that Christopher was not after all a saint was a blow to those who were inordinately attached to him. But it wasn't a fatal blow. Those of us who carried that little plastic statue of St. Chris' image on our dashboard weren't asked to remove it. The church didn't say St. Christopher hadn't existed, only that there simply wasn't enough evidence to establish his sainthood.

Why do I and countless others like St. Chris so much? Because we identify with him. He encourages us by showing us that God can use whatever we give him, even though what we have to give may seem insignificant by the world's standards.

Christopher lived in Greece sometime in the third century. Historically, that's nearly all we know about him. The stories surrounding his life are legendary—but no less inspiring to anyone who has ever struggled with self-worth than if they were verifiable.

It is said that Christopher was a giant of a man, a Paul Bunyan figure with a heart to match. He wanted nothing more than to lead a life pleasing to God. For years, he prayed that God would reveal to him how he might best use his life in God's service. But God was silent. A man of action, Christopher took matters into his own hands. He set off to a distant land to confer with a monk who was famous for his deep wisdom, holy life, and closeness to God.

Legend has it that after a long journey, the good man arrived at the monastery and arranged to meet with this holy monk. "Brother," he said, "I've come a great distance to ask you how I might best serve God and my neighbor."

The monk promised to pray for an answer to Christopher's question. Upon doing so, he returned to the pilgrim and told him, "Son, you can join our monastery and spend your life in prayer, fasting, and self-denial. This will please God."

The young man shook his head. "Brother, I am a man of large appetites, and I am not good with words. Please return to your prayer and dig deeper into God's will for my life." The good and holy monk did as he was asked, returning to Christopher only after days of contemplation. "Nearby," he said, "is a dangerous and fast-moving river. Many travelers come to it each day and find themselves unable to cross it because they are weak or sick or disabled, or sometimes simply because they are frightened of its dangers. With your great size and strength, you could easily carry them across. In this special way, you would serve and please God."

Christopher was delighted. This was the way he could finally use his gifts and better the world. He built a small hut near the river and happily spent his days carrying the weak and broken across the waters. At last, he had found his niche.

One day toward the end of his life, Christopher heard a tiny knock on his door. A small child was outside. "Sir," said the child, "I have no way across the river unless you help." The big man smiled, lovingly swept the child up into his arms and onto his shoulder, and started across the river.

But with every step, the child grew heavier and heavier on Christopher's back. It required every ounce of the man's strength to safely reach the opposite side. At last, exhausted, he put the child down on dry land. Puzzled, he asked the lad about the strange occurrence. The child replied, "My weight is great, sir, because I am the child Jesus. I carry the weight within me of all the weak and broken people you have assisted across the river during your years of service." With these words, he disappeared.

In Christian art, whether the plastic statue on the dashboard or the medal around the neck, St. Christopher is always shown with a child on his shoulder as he fords the river. The literal translation of his name is "Christ-bearer."

Was there really a St. Christopher? Did he carry the Christ child across the river? Does it matter? Legend or truth, and much better than a statue that weeps or bleeds, his story has the power to help us understand the meaning of our lives. It is the story of everyone who makes the most out of the gifts God has bestowed.

Each of us has a unique and much needed part to play in God's plan for bringing about his kingdom in this world. Some of us are called to be the holy monk; some are called to be a St. Christopher.

CHAPTER THREE

A Tale of Two Priests

Fr. Emery Blanchard was my pastor from the time I was eleven. When God created this man, he must have been thinking, *This one I'm going to send into the world with the least amount of gifts and see what he can do with them.*

Shy and retiring, Fr. Blanchard wasn't blessed with great social skills or a charismatic personality. He often struggled to find the right words to say. His parishioners agonized with him each Sunday as he painfully stuttered his way through his homily. Conversations with him were always one-sided. Though I grew up in his parish, I don't recall ever seeing him laugh or joke or just be playful. He often smiled, but I remember him as serious and solemn. When it came to administrating the parish's affairs, he would throw up his hands.

Fr. Blanchard wasn't entirely helpless or inept, but sometimes his demeanor gave that impression. When it did, his parishioners would flock to his side, offering their help and expertise.

When it came to obvious gifts, Fr. Blanchard had few. Yet thousands of us who knew him would say without hesitation that he was the most impressive priest we have ever known. People loved him. His parish flourished. Gentle and humble, he was truly the presence of Christ in our midst. Though they were few, his words always lifted us up. (He even found good things to say about me!) His humble and self-effacing ways rallied people around him and inspired their generosity. He empowered others to serve and give of themselves.

Fr. Blanchard gave us the gift of himself. Whether at a grade school soccer game, a parish picnic, a church decorating party, or a meeting of the men's club, he was always there smiling and nodding his head in approval. A man of great compassion, he came by to stop and awkwardly pray with those who were sick. He saw to it that families under financial duress received groceries. If one of his parishioners' kids was thrown in jail, he stopped by during visiting hours. Fr. Blanchard's door was open and his shoulder available twenty-four hours a day.

He never wrote a book or appeared on television. He was never mentioned as "bishop material," never listed among the city's movers and shakers, never received any awards. But then, come to think about it, neither did Jesus. Fr. Blanchard was simply the most Christlike man many of us had ever met. He may not have had an abundance of overt gifts, but he made a difference in our lives with the ones that he did have.

That's why it was standing room only at his funeral.

The funeral for Fr. "X," in the same week, was a different story.

When God created Fr. X, he took one of every gift off the shelf of heaven's storeroom and bestowed it on the man. Fr. X was a gifted orator with a sparkling personality. He was a leader of people, a champion of causes, an administrator without equal, and an organizer who could get things done. He had charm, wit, and a manner about him that just warmed up a room. He was electric. He was brilliant.

But then, suddenly, the fire went out. God alone knows why. I knew Fr. X well, but his withdrawal from the priesthood and from life remains a mystery to me. Alcohol became his refuge and his only friend. His gifts lay unused.

I've often thought that if Fr. X had died before the fire went out, no church would have been large enough to hold the mourners. He had touched so many with his gifts as a young priest. But the flames died, and in the end, less than a dozen people came to remember him at his funeral.

Nine times out of ten my Sunday Mass homily reflects on and applies the day's Scripture readings to the lives of the people in the pews, but sometimes something weighs so heavily on my little mind that I stray from that norm. The Sunday after the funerals for Fr. Blanchard and Fr. "X," my mind was filled with thoughts about them, and my homily spoke to the differences in their lives and the way their lives were remembered.

After one of the Masses that morning, a friend and parishioner came up to me and said, "Father, I was distracted all during Mass this morning wondering how many people will attend your funeral." My face must have betrayed my surprise, because she quickly added, "Hey, Father, you can count on my being there." Her remark made those two funerals very personal for me.

Attendance at a person's funeral cannot always be equated with the impact of that person's life—I've been to plenty of packed funerals for young people, including infants. People come not for the one who died but for themselves and for those who are left behind, to comfort or to find comfort in the face of great tragedy. They come seeking spiritual healing.

I've also been to many poorly attended funerals of truly great and wonderful people who have lived long, meaningful, and loving lives. Perhaps they had retired years before and lost contact with people; their friends had died, moved away, or simply couldn't get about anymore because of age or illness.

But to this day I believe that the difference in the attendance at the funerals for these two priests was indeed a reflection of how they impacted the lives of those who knew them.

That gives me pause. How do I use my gifts? How will I be remembered?

How will you?

CHAPTER FOUR

The Checkbook and the Soul

One morning before the beginning of the school day, Annie stopped me as I walked by her locker. "I've got something for you," she said, and pulled an envelope with my name on it out of her locker. Inside was $12.50. When I looked puzzled, Annie said, "Hey, Father, let's start another miracle." When I finally made the connection, I smiled and gave her a big hug.

The day before, Annie and her sophomore classmates had come together in the chapel for a prayer service. The center-piece of the service had been a Scripture reading from John 6, in which St. John tells the story about Jesus feeding five thousand people with only two fish and five loaves of bread. Wondrously, after everyone had eaten, twelve baskets of food remained!

This story is found in all four Gospels, but only St. John mentions that the original five loaves and two fish were the generous gift of a little boy. Our prayer service had high-lighted that little boy's actions. His gift, as modest as it was in the face of the hunger of five thousand people, was seed for the miracle. To bring home this point, I had hung a banner in the chapel that read, "Let's start a miracle."

At the end of the service, each of the sophomores had signed up for a service project. With her gift, Annie was taking the message and her service commitment to heart. When I asked her why $12.50, she told me it was 10 percent of her candy winnings. Every year our students participate in a candy sale that funds student activities for the school, and this year Annie had been awarded $125.00 as the top salesperson. The $12.50 she had given me was the Biblical 10 percent tithe.

An old proverb says, "Show me a man's checkbook and I'll tell you the state of his soul." This was certainly true of Annie's checkbook. I don't know where she learned to give 10 percent of her treasure. It may have been in church; it may have been at home. Maybe her own reading and reflections on the spirituality of giving had prompted her gift. Wherever she learned to give back to God, it was now a part of her character. I suspect that if we looked into Annie's checkbook today, we would see she's still giving 10 percent of her treasure.

Twelve dollars and fifty cents is not a lot of money in the face of today's gas and grocery prices. But then, five loaves of bread and two puny fish was not a lot of food for five thousand hungry people. Annie and the little boy in the gospel story made the most out of what they had been given by God. God's miracles start with us.

CHAPTER FIVE

Carpe Diem

Luke was in my first period sophomore religion class years back. This young man always had a smile on his face. He was upbeat, honest to the core, and could take a reprimand without sulking. I liked him a lot. Respected by his teachers and well-liked by his classmates, Luke had one glaring fault: he was always late. I think God had set his internal clock five minutes behind the rest of the world. I used to kid him that he would be late for his own funeral.

One Monday morning the bell rang at eight o'clock to signal the beginning of first period. The student taking attendance came over to my desk and said, "Hey, Father, everybody is here except Luke. Should I mark him absent?"

"No," I said, "Luke is always late. He'll be here."

As she left to put the attendance sheet on the classroom door, we heard a terrible noise coming from the street two floors below our classroom window: screeching brakes, a scream, a thud, and the breaking of glass. We ran to the window to see what had happened. Below us, Luke lay flat on his back in the middle of the street, blood pooling by his head.

We learned later that Luke had been running behind that Monday morning. His mom had dropped him off across the street from the high school. He jumped out of the car, slammed the door, and raced across the street without looking. One of our seniors didn't see him in time, and the front of her car hit Luke. He flew up in the air, bounced off her windshield, and rolled off the hood to the street, badly injured.

I raced down the stairs and made my way through the crowd of people around Luke, all of them trying to make him comfortable. Taking his hand, I did the only thing I could think of: I prayed. When the ambulance came, one of the medics asked me to ride to the hospital with Luke. "Sometimes a familiar face is good medicine," he said. "Keep talking to him. Make sure he stays conscious."

I'll never forget what Luke said to me during that scary ride when I asked him what had gone through his mind right after he was hit. "Father," he said, his words halting, "I kept looking up at the school windows. When I saw all those kids staring down at me, all I could think of was how lucky they were to be in class."

Sometimes we have to be in the shoes of somebody like Luke, on the verge of never having another Monday to complain about, in order to appreciate the gift and treasure that every Monday is in our lives.

The last thing God did before pushing us out into the world was to insert in each of us a time clock and then wind it up. He wound each of our clocks individually, with a distinct and different tension. God wound some of our clocks so tightly that they are going to tick away with life for a hundred years. Others will run out of ticks after seventy years. God wound some clocks so loosely that time runs out after only fifteen years—or less.

Only God knows how many Monday mornings we have left on this earth. To throw away a day while we're eagerly waiting for the weekend—or retirement or vacation or graduation or whatever—is about as foolish and wasteful a thing as one can do in life. Who is to say what opportunities or treasures a particular Monday has in store for us? (Did you know that Albert Einstein discovered his theory of relativity on the electrodynamics of moving bodies and equivalence of mass and mechanical energy on a Monday? Well, I don't know for sure it was a Monday, but it could have been!)

Our most valuable possession is the gift of our life. We squander that precious gift when we let ourselves get bored, when we wish the day was over instead of looking for its treasures.

Imagine that some very rich benefactor approached you with this promise: every night as you slept, he would slip into your bedroom and place a gift box containing fourteen hundred dollars at the foot of your bed. He promised that he would continue to do this every night for the rest of your life. He had only one condition: you had to spend all of that money, every day, before the day was through. Whatever you failed to spend would go back to him and be lost to you.

Only a fool wouldn't spend every last dollar, every day, of that generous gift.

Does this scenario sound farfetched? It's not. Every one of us is the recipient of just such a gift, and it sits there every morning at the foot of our bed when we wake up. The benefactor is God, and the fourteen hundred units in the gift box are not dollars but minutes—enough to equal twenty-four hours. One day. Perhaps a Monday. If we don't use those precious minutes, they are lost to us forever.

How can we remember to make the most of each day? It helps me to think back to that Monday morning with Luke.

I've also purchased a beautiful picture of a sunrise with these words of the eighteenth-century German poet Johann Wolfgang von Goethe etched beneath it: "Nothing should be more highly prized than the value of each day." The picture hangs on the wall next to my door. On those mornings when I'm tempted to wish the day was already over, I touch those words on my way out and try to make them mine. It works!

CHAPTER SIX

Today Builds Tomorrow

In 1985, Pope John Paul II visited Vancouver, British Columbia, in Canada. On the first evening of his visit, he was scheduled to host and speak at a rally for young people. Since Seattle is only 130 miles away, I decided to take a delegation from our high school. About 150 of our students and chaperones boarded buses and made the trip for the evening rally. Our time could not have been better spent.

As I walked to my office the next day at school, I found my door blocked by a huge sign—a Washington state freeway direction sign, eight feet wide and three feet tall. On a green background, the white letters read "Papal Visit." I recognized it as one of the signs we had passed on the highway as we bused to see the pope. On the return trip, a van full of seniors had decided the sign would be a great souvenir. Before propping it against my door, they'd all signed it on the back and attached a note that read, "Hey, Father! The pope was cool." (I hope and pray that the statute of limitations has run out, because that sign is still in my office today.)

The pope's message to the sixty-five thousand young people squeezed into Vancouver's stadium had both described and challenged them. He began by reading these words from St. Luke's Gospel:

I will show you what someone is like who comes to me, listens to my words, and acts on them. That one is like a person building a house, who dug deeply and laid the foundation on rock; when the flood came, the river burst against that house but could not shake it because it had been well built. But the one who listens and does not act is like a person who built a house on the ground without a foundation. When the river burst against it, it collapsed at once and was completely destroyed.

LUKE 6:47-49

Pope John Paul made these powerful words come alive for his teenage audience as he described the foundation they were building for their entire future in this critical stage of their life. If they built their foundation on rock, as Jesus pointed out in the Gospel, they would suffer no damage when the floods came. If, however, they built on soil without a foundation, when the floods came collapse would be inevitable, and they would be washed away.

The pope's message reminds me of a wonderful story about a rich man, equally wealthy in compassion, who approached a carpenter in his town who was struggling to find work. The rich man put this proposition to the poor carpenter: he would put one million dollars at the carpenter's disposal, and in turn, the young worker would build a magnificent mansion for the rich man.

They shook hands on the deal.

The carpenter was good at his trade, but he was not an honest man. He knew that if he used second-rate materials and cut corners in the construction of the rich man's house, he could save a great deal of money—money that he could pocket. The shoddy workmanship could be covered up, and the rich man would never know about it.

When the carpenter finished the home, it looked beautiful. He alone knew that within a few years the homeowner would be hounded with problems due to the inferior materials he'd used and his poor workmanship.

When the rich man arrived to inspect the newly constructed house, he was very pleased. Then came the surprise. He reached into his pocket and removed the title to the house. "Here," he said to the carpenter, "this house is yours. For years, I've felt sorry for you and your family living without a home of your own. I want to give you this house so that you may live out your life in it."[1]

Whether we are in high school or entering retirement, each day that God gives us is another step in the construction of our life. If we cut corners, if our efforts are halfhearted, we might cover it up for a time, but eventually we—and those around us—will suffer from our poor workmanship. Would any of us want to be the patient of a surgeon who cheated his way through medical school? Would any of us want to be a passenger in a plane whose pilot slept through the courses on navigation? Would any of us want to sit down to a meal prepared by a chef who skipped over the sections in culinary school on hygiene?

Not that constructing our lives with integrity is easy. Both teenagers and retired folks are often told, "These are the best years of your lives!" But for some teenagers, high school is anything but "the best years of their lives." Some suffer painfully from feelings of low self-worth, loneliness, fear of failure, and rejection. Retirement offers similar challenges to older adults. To those who suffer painfully from inadequate income, health limitations, loneliness, and rejection, retirement feels nothing like "the best years of their lives." Yet few teenagers would give up their years in high school, and most older adults prefer retirement to the alternative.

I've often asked my students if they would be willing to forego high school in exchange for ten million dollars, tax free. A few students always say they would take the money and skip the years, but most say, "No way!" The friendships, lessons, challenges, and even the mistakes of high school are too valuable. They wouldn't put those up for sale at any price. These kids know that such experiences are the building materials out of which they are made.

Pope John Paul's message that night at the youth rally up in Vancouver was this: what you do today will determine the quality of your tomorrow. His words were not just for the young. They speak to all of us.

SECTION TWO

"Hey, Father!
What Does God Look Like?"

CHAPTER SEVEN

Unlikely Angels

It was a week before Christmas. The bus was filled with the noise and chaos that only twenty-eight freshman boys can create. We were returning from a wrestling meet, yet another loss in a long string for my team. As usual, the team had taken the loss hard—for about twelve seconds.

The meet had finished later than expected, and it was way past dinnertime as I drove our bus out of the little town of Snohomish that December night. Stomachs rumbling, the boys began to plead with me to find a restaurant for a dinner stop.

Now, I know firsthand what twenty-eight young boys can do to a restaurant, so I ignored them and kept driving. But it was Christmas, and when they began to chant in unison, "Priest brutality," my heart melted. I pulled the bus into the parking lot of the next restaurant along the freeway and prayed the boys would be on their best behavior.

When we trooped in the door, the cafe staff exchanged nervous glances. Some of the patrons asked for their checks and headed for the doors. But a restaurant isn't a church, and I couldn't ask twenty-eight teen boys not to talk. When you have that many boys in one confined space for a meal, you simply have to expect a certain level of noise, motion, and play. And sure enough, while we waited for our meal to be served, the boys built castles out of the salt and pepper shakers, constructed pea shooters out of the paper placemats, and experimented with the catsup to see who could come up with the worst looking face wound.

Two disapproving waitresses began to serve the boys their pizzas. As the team surveyed the food and jockeyed for position, a student yelled over the din—loud enough to be heard clearly back at the high school—"Hey, Father! Say grace so we can eat."

The chaos suddenly ceased. It was a marvelous moment, a powerful moment, a Christmas moment. The restaurant became all at once a veritable oasis of peace, calm, and spirituality as quiet settled gently over the room. It was as if we had entered the eye of a hurricane. Mothers in the neighboring booths quieted their children. Waitresses froze in their tracks. Men removed their baseball caps, and the sounds of a busy restaurant came to a halt. Every head in the place turned and fixed on those twenty-eight freshman boys as they momentarily stopped fooling around and bowed their little heads for grace.

Embarrassed by all the attention, I wanted to crawl underneath the table and out of sight. Instead, I prayed in a loud voice for God to bless our pizzas. When the last word of the blessing faded, my young saints-for-a-moment returned to their banter, grabbing slices of pizza and crying out, "Who has the pepperoni?"

Boys don't eat pizza, they inhale it. When they had consumed every last scrap, including the crusts, I went over to the counter to pay the bill. To my surprise, the hostess told me that someone had already paid our tab, including the tip. When I asked who, the hostess pointed to an older gentleman sitting in a booth by himself near the back.

Grateful, but puzzled, I went over to thank him. We talked for a few minutes. He asked where we were from, curious about what kind of a school prompted kids to say grace in public before having pizza. When I told him that we were a Catholic school, he simply nodded. I asked him what had prompted his generosity, and he mumbled something about "it being Christmas and all." But I thought I saw tears in his eyes.

I thanked him again, and then shepherded my young flock out of the restaurant and back onto the bus for the trip home.

Three weeks later, a letter arrived at school addressed to "the priest in charge of the wrestling team." It was from our benefactor in the restaurant. It read in part, "Father, three weeks ago you thanked me for what I did for you and the boys. I couldn't find the words that night, but it was I who wanted to thank all of you." He went on to explain that he was a Catholic who hadn't seen the inside of a church since the baptism of his second child nearly sixty years before. What he had witnessed in the restaurant that night brought back memories of the time when he, too, had been fifteen—a time when prayer, faith, and church had been a very meaningful part of his life. He didn't share with me why he had abandoned these spiritual anchors, but he did say that our prayer had rekindled in him a hunger to sit at the table of faith once again. He wanted us to know that he had attended Mass on Christmas, and that he had every intention of reconnecting with his forgotten and abandoned faith. He ended by asking me to thank the boys for their gift.

As I read the man's letter, I tried to remember what might have impacted that elderly gentleman so much. I suspect that it was more than the thirty seconds of grace my boys had paused for. The kids might have been loud and boisterous in their laughter and bantering, but they were also genuinely enjoying one another. They may have made the patrons and the staff a bit nervous by their sheer numbers, but they were respectful to one another, and their smiles and responses to others in the restaurant were warm and inviting. They were good kids and their goodness was evident.

I think our benefactor had made a connection between their goodness and the role of prayer and faith in their lives. I think he realized that their prayer that night was a genuine desire to thank God for the unexpected meal and those they shared it with. He must have realized that for these boys, prayer wasn't some kind of religious punctuation, like starting each sentence with a capital letter. Watching and listening to them had spurred him to examine his life and go in search of something he had once found important but long ago lost.

The next day I took his letter to wrestling practice and read it to the team. The boys sat in unusual silence, stunned that they could be a source of inspiration to anyone, let alone to some elderly gentleman who had been so moved by them that he'd bought their dinners. Their surprise was surpassed only by my own sense of awe in a God who could choose a group of rambunctious boys as his angels, sending them on a mission to retrieve one of his lost sheep.

CHAPTER EIGHT

Casting a Shadow

On my first day in my new parish at St. Matthew's, I received a call from a very worried mother whose son, Chad, had been in a serious accident two days earlier. A seventh-grade student in the parish grade school, Chad had been running headlong from the classroom to the play field for recess. Unfortunately, he didn't see the cyclone fence that had recently been put up as a protection against traffic, and he folded over the waist-high fence like a limp French fry, rupturing his spleen.

I went to see Chad, but my attempts to connect with him seemed futile. I couldn't tell whether he was depressed, frightened, or just shy, but during my fifteen-minute visit I got a total of two soft mumbles and one labored "yes" out of him. Finally I prayed the prayers of our church over him, wished him well, and backed out of his room feeling like a complete failure.

It took me years to realize it, but I was far from a failure in Chad's eyes. Our lives intersected often during the next ten years. He attended and graduated from the high school I work in, and during college and his first years in a career, we ran into each other frequently. I never heard it directly from him, but I often heard from his family and friends how important my hospital visit had been to him. One of his teachers in high school showed me a paper Chad had written about "The People I Most Admire." I was high on his list because of that hospital visit that I'd thought was a failure. My prayers and my words of cheer had barely registered with him, but my presence

43

at a vulnerable and frightening time in his young life told him that he wasn't alone, he hadn't been forgotten, and he was loved and valued. That spiritual medicine was every bit as healing as the prescriptions he was being fed through the IV tubes.

Consoling a friend who has lost a loved one or visiting someone with a serious or terminal illness often leaves us at a loss for words. Sometimes we don't even try. We forget that our presence is more important than any words we might speak and will be remembered long after our words have been forgotten. Our presence has a decided effect on the well-being and even the healing of those we visit.

Presence is more than just a warm body taking up space. Presence communicates a message of deep caring and a willingness to be there for others in their need. Praying for others, providing home-cooked meals, even simply sitting quietly at a bedside stroking someone's hand says, "I care. You are not alone."

In the Acts of the Apostles, St. Luke describes a thought-provoking scene that conveys how our presence can offer caring, love, and faith to others. The time was shortly after Pentecost, and St. Peter had just arrived in Jerusalem. His presence caused great excitement among the Christians there. Many of them gathered up their sick and those possessed by demons and placed them on stretchers and cots along the streets they knew St. Peter would have to pass. They did this, in the hope that Peter's shadow would fall on the sick and heal them (see Acts 5:15).

Can a person's presence and the shadow he or she casts heal broken lives? I've seen it time and time again. Our shadow has the power to change lives, inspire lives, and mend lives. It also, unfortunately, has the power to harm lives.

Jesus reserved some of his harshest criticism for hypocrites: "Whoever causes one of these little ones who believe to sin, it would be better for him if a great millstone were put around his neck and he were thrown into the sea" (Mark 9:42). We've all heard stories of those whose faith lives have been seriously harmed by hypocritical religious leaders whose presence and shadow caused great harm in the lives of their followers. Some ten years ago my parish began a program to welcome back Catholics who had abandoned their faith, or perhaps more accurately, their church. Often these refugees from an earlier faith, when encouraged to tell why they had left the church, mentioned a priest who had not been there for them. Religious leaders who fail to "walk their talk" can do real harm.

You don't have to be a religious leader to cast a shadow that either deepens or injures others' spiritual lives, though. When the fabled Knute Rockne first arrived at Notre Dame, where he coached football from 1918 to 1930, he was neither a Catholic nor a very serious Christian. This was soon to change. He would become one of the most fervent, dedicated, and loyal of Catholics—thanks to a shadow cast by others. Like many stories about famous people, I'm not sure how much of this one is factual, but it certainly is inspirational.

According to the story, shortly after Rockne became Notre Dame's head coach, he noticed something strange about his players. On game days they would leave their hotel rooms very early in the morning, before breakfast, in groups of two or three. This meant they were losing those extra hours of sleep so coveted by college students on Saturday mornings. They never talked about where they had been, and since it wasn't against team rules, Rockne said nothing.

One Saturday morning the coach decided to follow some of his players to satisfy his growing curiosity about these excursions. He discovered they were attending early morning Mass at a nearby Catholic church in order to ask God's help in keeping them injury-free and making them a credit to their faith during the game. The coach wanted to be supportive of what he considered a healthy practice, so he started attending Mass with them. After a few years of this, he began to feel a spiritual hunger of his own. To be able to fully participate in the Mass and the Eucharist, he joined the Catholic Church.

A wonderful proverb in the Christian family says, "Be mindful of your words and deeds. They may be the only Bible that some will ever read."

What kind of a shadow do we cast? Are others' lives better off because we have passed by?

CHAPTER NINE

Giving God a Human Face

One of the perks of being a Catholic priest is that little children often mistake us for God. When I stand outside the church after a Sunday morning Mass, I can almost count on some small child coming up to me and saying, "Hi, God!" That's tonic for my ego, especially because the child's parents often think I am the furthest thing from God on the planet.

It makes sense, when you think about it, that children mistake priests for God. When parents pack kids off to church on a Sunday morning, they usually tell them something like, "We're going to church to spend time with God; that's why you're wearing your best clothes and must be on your best behavior." When the youngster gets to church and starts looking around for God, it's no contest. It has to be the priest. He's wearing all those colorful and unusual vestments, he's standing in the center of all the people and he's doing all the talking. Who else could possibly be God?

One of my favorite experiences of mistaken divine identity took place in my very first parish assignment. I was standing outside the church after Sunday Mass, greeting the departing parishioners, kissing their babies, and generally trying to make myself likable. A little girl came up to me and said, "How did you get down?" I didn't understand her question and stood there looking dumb. She grabbed a handful of my vestments and pulled me into the church, where she pointed up to the large crucifix in the sanctuary. She wanted to know how I had gotten down off that cross!

"Hey, Father!"

As children get older, they no longer mistake me for God. But their fascination with putting a human face on God continues. I love the story about the little boy who was busy drawing with his crayons at the kitchen table. His mother looked over and said, "What are you drawing?" Without looking up from his work, the lad replied, "I'm drawing a picture of God." The mother said, "But, Son, that's impossible. No one knows what God looks like." The boy replied, "Well, they will when I'm finished!"

I used to think this desire of little children to see God's face was cute, but certainly something they would grow out of as their minds matured and they became more capable of understanding theological concepts like the nature of God. I no longer dismiss the hunger of children to see God's face as a mark of immaturity. It was a little girl who helped me change my view.

It was a typically wet and windy Seattle Sunday morning. Standing outside the church greeting departing parishioners, I was anxious to get back inside where it was warm, but the unwritten code of the Catholic priesthood dictated that I set an example for cheerful suffering. So there I was, cheerfully enduring the chill as the wind slapped the vestments into my face, with a bright word of encouragement for everyone who filed out of the nine o'clock Sunday Mass.

I noticed a woman and a little girl coming out the doors, the girl's hand tightly clutching her mother's. They headed straight toward me. At first, I was sure the young lady was going to hand me one of the church envelopes from the rack in the pews and show me a picture she had drawn on it during Mass. As they drew near, however, I was relieved to see there was no envelope; I wouldn't be embarrassed (yet again) by failing to recognize what the child had drawn.

They stopped in front of me. "Father," the woman said, "my daughter has a question for you." I had the uneasy feeling from her manner that I had better come up with the right answer or there would be consequences. I said, "What is it, sweetheart?" Shyly, she said, "What does God look like?" With a mischievous twinkle in my eye, I answered, "Well, God looks just like me."

Have you ever noticed that sometimes when you're trying to be funny or cute with youngsters, your words fall flat? This was one of those times. The little girl's face fell in disappointment at my answer. Her mother's face showed that she was not amused. Sensing my mistake, I recovered quickly and said, "I was just kidding. If you really want to know what God looks like, go home and do something kind for your family. Then go and look in a mirror. When you do something kind, you look like God."

Her face lit up and she nodded knowingly. I also made some points with her mother, who told me as they left, "You did much better on your second try." The two happily went off, hand in hand, to the coffee hour, and I headed back into the church with a much-needed reminder that when a child asks you for bread, you don't hand her a stone.

My answer wasn't just an attempt to please the girl or win points with her mother. I was trying to explain to her that God's face is the face of love. We experience the presence of God when we receive or give the warmth of love. First John 4:12 says this beautifully: "No one has ever seen God. Yet, if we love one another, God remains in us, and his love is brought to perfection in us."

A little story that has been around a long time captures the heart of how we experience God's presence—how we see God's face:

"Hey, Father!"

Two brothers inherited their father's wheat farm. They divided the land equally and each built a home on his half of the property. One brother had a wife and five children; the other brother was single. The brothers loved each other very much.

A very strange and puzzling thing happened every year after the wheat was harvested and stored in the brothers' separate barns. The married brother, worried that his single brother had no children to take care of him when he got old, would get up in the middle of the night, fill a wagon with wheat, and secretly take it to his brother's barn. He figured the income from the extra wheat would provide for his brother's care when he could no longer work. Yet, no matter how much of his wheat he secretly gave his brother, his own supply never diminished!

Then one dark night on his way across the fields, he crossed paths with his brother—who was, like him, transporting a wagon full of wheat. Instantly he knew what had been happening. All the time he had been filling his brother's barn, his brother, concerned about his having enough income to provide for his wife and children, had been filling his.

Moved beyond words, the brothers ran and embraced each other. Later, they built a small shrine on the spot where they had embraced. They called it "sacred ground" because it was a place where God had stood; it was where they had seen God's face in each other.[2]

What does God look like? Look in the mirror after you have loved. God looks exactly like you!

CHAPTER TEN

Choosing Life

The school secretary softly knocked on the classroom door. I could see her through the little window and knew she wouldn't be interrupting a class unless it was important. She handed me a telephone message marked "Urgent." It was from a student who had graduated the year before. She was in the hospital.

I rushed to a phone, thinking she had probably been in an accident and wanted me to come and administer the sacrament of the anointing. Her voice sounded healthy enough, and as we exchanged greetings I grew increasingly curious and puzzled about why her message was marked "Urgent."

But then she said, "Hey, Father! I just gave birth to the most beautiful baby yesterday. I've arranged to have him adopted and tomorrow his new parents are coming to pick him up. Can you be here and pray a blessing over us?" I had known Rebecca all through her high school years and liked her a great deal. But even if I hadn't known her, I would have readily accepted.

I wanted to talk with Rebecca privately, so I arrived at the hospital a good hour before the time we had set for the blessing ceremony. Actually, it wasn't so much that I wanted to talk to her as it was the feeling that she needed to talk to me— someone from her religious family—about her pregnancy and her decision to give up her baby for adoption.

When I walked into her room, she was dressed and sitting

in the chair next to her hospital bed. In her arms was her child. The baby was beautiful and so was his eighteen-year-old mother. As we talked, my admiration for Rebecca grew. She had always been a young lady of good character, guiding her life and choices with Christian values. She acknowledged that she and her boyfriend had made a poor choice one night, not thinking through the consequences.

When they discovered that they were "with child," these two young parents-to-be were scared and overwhelmed by the changes and challenges a child would bring to their lives. Were they even close to being ready for marriage and parenthood? What of their dreams for college? How would their families react? With each question, there were more fears, doubts, and uncertainties.

Both young people were fortunate to have loving and supportive parents. With their help and guidance, Rebecca and her boyfriend explored the choices that lay before them. In the end, after honestly and sometimes painfully assessing their maturity and ability to care for their child, they decided to put him up for adoption. Rebecca never considered abortion. "Father, I know our church teaches that abortion is wrong," she told me, "but I don't need the church to tell me that. I know in my heart a child in the womb is God's work."

Her boyfriend didn't agree, and their emotional discussions over this issue opened her eyes to a significant difference in their values. It also ended their relationship, and she told me that he would not be present for the blessing ceremony. The tears in her eyes were witness to how difficult the past few months had been for her. Now, it was time for the blessing ceremony.

The hospital chapel was tiny, barely able to contain Rebecca

and her baby son, the adoptive parents, the agency represen-
tative, a nurse, Rebecca's parents, and me. We began with our
church's blessing on the newborn child, thanking God for the
gift of his life. We then prayed for Rebecca as she held the
child in her arms, asking God to give her peace with the decision that she had made. Finally, we offered blessing and prayer
for the adoptive parents, thanking God for their generosity
and their willingness to accept this child into their lives.

When the blessings were concluded, Rebecca addressed
her child's new mother and father. She thanked them for wel-
coming her child into their lives and home. She then placed
her baby in their arms. I couldn't help but notice that there
were tears in every eye in that small chapel, including my own.
We watched in silence, each with our own thoughts, as the
adoptive parents walked out the front doors of the hospital
with their child. As they did, I wrapped my arms around
Rebecca and whispered in her ear, "You're one of my heroes."

My church has always been strongly pro-life. But like
Rebecca, I don't need my church to tell me what to think
about abortion. At the very core of what I believe and value is
the sanctity of human life, from the womb to the tomb. I
respect those who see this issue differently, and I am bothered
a great deal by the lack of respect that some on the pro-life
side show to those who choose abortion. I no longer attend
pro-life rallies. The name-calling, anger, graphic pictures, and,
yes, occasional violence are not marks of people who sincerely
believe in the sanctity of all life. How can one champion the
sacredness of the child in the womb on one hand while on the
other attacking and treating as anything *but* sacred the lives of
those who disagree with them?

In my mind, Rebecca made the right choice. She didn't make it after listening to a debate on abortion. She didn't make it in the midst of hateful rhetoric, catchy phrases, graphic pictures, and waving signs. She didn't make it after carefully weighing our church's teachings. She listened to her heart and to the quiet voice of God, who makes his home within us.

Our Christian Scriptures tell us that the Spirit of God dwells within each of us (see 1 Corinthians 3:16). God's Spirit doesn't live within us because he has no place better to hang out. He's not there as some kind of divine decoration. God's Spirit lives within us as a consultant, a counselor, and a source of wisdom for us to tap into as we seek to make the right choices. This was the role of the Spirit of God within the early disciples of Jesus (see Acts 6:3), and this is the role of the Spirit of God today. God spoke to Moses from the burning bush; God spoke to Rebecca from her heart.

Rebecca's quiet decision to listen to God led her to give life to her baby. Her choice and her story witness more powerfully to the sanctity of life in the womb than any march, rally, or campaign. Every time she tells her story, God's message of life comes through.

CHAPTER ELEVEN

God Loves Stories

Preaching on Sundays can be a hard business. Listening to preaching on Sundays can be even harder. There have been times I thought I had a riveting sermon that would capture even a gnat's attention, only to look out at the pews and see a foggy daze descending over my congregation.

Preaching must have been tough for Jesus, too, although at least the people of his time did not measure him by what they saw on television and in the movies. There's no question that he was an effective preacher. Who else could get five thousand people to follow him out to the shores of Tiberias—without their lunch—so they could soak up his words (see John 6:1)?

One of the keys to Jesus' success as a preacher was his skill as a storyteller. He and God the Father must have put their heads together and decided that stories were the best way to penetrate our thick skulls, because Jesus told some dandies. I don't doubt that the Father loved Jesus' stories—after all, he was prominently featured in all of them.

Perhaps the most memorable and popular of Jesus' stories is the story of the Prodigal Son. The reason for its popularity is simple: It isn't just a story we read or hear, it's one that we live, just about every day.

One windy and very wet afternoon I was driving on the freeway, heading toward the Evergreen Point floating bridge that empties into Seattle. Traffic was bumper to bumper, a fairly typical condition on a rainy day. My leg was beginning to cramp from putting constant pressure on the brake. The HOV (high occupancy vehicle) lane, on my right, constantly tempted me. The cars with two or more people aboard, entitled to use that lane, zipped right past the rest of us.

With nothing to do but stare ahead at the endless sea of brake lights as I massaged my cramping leg, I monitored the cars in the HOV lane. Occasionally I spotted a cheater, and I would offer a prayer that God would position a police officer up ahead to bring him to justice, both civil and divine.

As traffic nears the entrance to the bridge, the HOV lane runs out, and the privileged few allowed to use it must merge into the lane that we common lemmings use. As I neared this merge point, a very large, very powerful, and very expensive Mercedes Benz shot by me in the car pool lane. The driver flipped on his blinker and attempted to merge into my lane about ten cars ahead of me. Normal courtesy would call for those drivers ahead to make a space and let the driver in. But there was a problem. The driver of the very important looking Mercedes was alone in his luxury car and had no business being in the HOV lane. The drivers ahead of me took note of this, closed ranks bumper to bumper and refused to let him in their lane. They were obviously saying that one who flaunts the laws of the road is not entitled to courtesy and respect. They were more than content to leave him in the dead-end car pool lane, alone in his sin and shame.

As my car crept up behind the Mercedes, I could see a look of desperation in the man's eyes, pleading with me to make a space for him. His signal light cried out for pity and forgiveness. In that moment of decision, I remembered Jesus' story of the Prodigal Son. It was being played out right in front of me.

Like the Prodigal Son, the driver of the Mercedes had chosen to leave the traffic family and its rules and responsibilities. He had chosen to enter the fast lane where he didn't belong, squandering and misusing his environmental inheritance by driving alone. Now that the fast lane had run out, he wanted to come back home and rejoin our little traffic family. You could see in his eyes that he knew he had sinned and was in need of mercy from those drivers who had played by the rules. But his plea was met by an unforgiving, angry, bumper-to-bumper line of older brothers who were offended by his reckless and selfish ways. They were certainly not of a mind to offer their sinful brother either welcome or forgiveness.

In this heavy, endless line of traffic, could there possibly be just one forgiving father figure, as there was in Jesus' story? Would one of us set aside our anger and resentment for this prodigal's behavior and welcome him into our lane? Would one of us order the fatted calf to be killed and a banquet of welcome prepared for this son who was lost and now is found? These questions circled through my head as my right front bumper slowly closed on his left rear bumper. Would I play the role of the older, unforgiving brother or would I choose the path of the generous and merciful father? Should I hit my brakes and wave him in, or should I close ranks like the drivers ahead?

How often life replays the story of the prodigal—and here it was right in front of me again. This universal story is as old as the fall from grace of Adam and Eve. Every time people hurt and offend us, we're confronted with a choice. Will we respond like the older brother or like the father?

God speaks to us through the stories of Jesus. I heard his

unmistakable voice that afternoon. If I wanted to sleep that night, I knew I had no choice. I did what God has done for me time and time again. I smiled and waved him in.

SECTION THREE

"Hey, Father!
Does God Ever Give Up on Us?"

CHAPTER TWELVE

Our Mistakes Are Not Fatal

A few years ago, I read in the paper that Roy Reigels had died at the age of eighty-five. If his name doesn't ring a bell with you, perhaps his nickname does: "Wrong Way Reigels." For most of his adult life, that's how many people remembered him. He picked up his unfortunate nickname because of fifteen infamous seconds in a football game.

On January 1, 1929, Georgia Tech and the University of California played each other in the Rose Bowl. Roy was a linebacker for California. In the closing minutes of the second quarter, Georgia Tech had the ball and was moving down the field. On third down, at about the fifty-yard line, a jarring tackle on the Georgia Tech running back popped the ball in the air. Roy Reigels snatched it, and with the interception tucked under his arm, started to run. He reversed direction several times, evading tackler after tackler, and finally headed for daylight.

With an open field in front of him and the roar of the capacity crowd in his ears, Roy raced for the goal line—the wrong goal line. He couldn't hear the panicked screams of his teammates as they chased after him. Frantic, they did what they had to do: they tackled their own player just a few yards short of the end zone.

Roy's mistake was not only embarrassing, it led to a Georgia Tech touchdown. Forcing California to give up the ball on a punt from their own end zone, Georgia ended up scoring their only touchdown of the game. They also scored the extra point—and won the game by a score of eight to seven.

The next day, newspapers across the country headlined Roy Reigels' mistake. Those fifteen seconds got more print than the drama of the entire game. They mockingly called him, "Wrong Way Reigels," an unkind name that stayed with him the rest of his life.

But one paper from Sacramento took a much different slant on Roy's mistake. Rather than focusing on Roy's wrong-way run, the reporter wrote a glowing story about Roy's efforts in the second half, calling those final thirty minutes of football the most inspiring and skilled ever played by a linebacker for the University of California. In this one article, Roy was a hero, not a goat.

How was Reigels able to play such an inspired second half after his embarrassing goof? Roy told the reporter that after his mistake, he was so humiliated he left the field, ran to the dressing room, hid behind the lockers, and started to cry. He stayed hidden when his team came in at halftime, unable to face them. When it came time for the team to go out for the second half, Coach Clarence Price called out the starting lineup. When he came to linebacker, he loudly called out Reigels' name.

With head hanging, Reigels came out from behind the lockers. "Coach, I can't go back in there after what happened. I let the team down and made a fool out of myself," he said. Coach Price replied, "Son, you made a bad mistake and it hurt us, but the game is only half over. We need you. Now, get out there!"[3]

Roy needed to hear those words. They told him the coach

believed in him and was counting on him to turn things around in the second half. This knowledge fueled his desire to give the final thirty minutes everything he had.

I see Roy's story in people like Marcie, a senior in one of my classes. Just before Christmas, I couldn't help but notice she seemed troubled. When I asked her about it, she hesitated, unsure she wanted to tell me. Then through her tears she told me she'd been arrested for shoplifting. She had been Christmas shopping with friends at the mall and had stolen some small cosmetic items. A security guard had caught her and called the police. She was given a citation to appear in court and then released to her parents. "Father, no one will ever trust me again," she agonized. "Especially my parents. I just want to die." Shame and disgrace hung over her like a dark cloud, and she was convinced that the sun would never shine again.

Marcie didn't know that all of us make mistakes, some much more serious than shoplifting. All of us fail. And when we do, it feels like the light has gone out in our world. Our self-esteem and our self-respect plummet. We feel lost in a forest of shame.

When we reach this point, we can learn something valuable from the story of Roy Reigels. Coach Clarence Price opened Roy's eyes to an important truth: one bad play doesn't determine the outcome of the game. One bad play doesn't define the player. Roy had a coach who believed in him and counted on him to rise above his mistake and play his heart out in the second half.

Jesus has played this role in my own life and in the life of countless others. He knows my mistakes, flaws, and sins better than anyone. But he also assures me that my mistakes are not fatal. Sin isn't a terminal disease. I can recover and go on to make something beautiful out of my life. God doesn't judge my life on the evidence of one dark, shameful moment. If he did, we would all be in trouble. The message of Jesus was one of redemption through the mercy and forgiveness of God. No matter how badly we have fallen, we can recover and begin anew.

When I was a youngster of eight or nine, I stole a quarter from my mother's purse. I don't remember the reason, but it was probably candy-related. I am sure that I enjoyed the momentary pleasure, but the taste of remorse, shame, and disgust at my sin lingered until I could no longer bear it. I went to my mother, and with tears pouring down my little cheeks, I confessed.

I no longer remember her words, but I do remember coming away from our talk feeling cleansed. The darkness lifted and I was determined to live up to her faith in me and my goodness. She also reminded me, drawing from her Irish faith, that now that I had made things right with her, I needed to make things right with God. I did and I felt wonderful.

I often tell this story to parish children at First Confession, the first time they acknowledge their sinfulness to God in the presence of a priest. I gather them together as a group, have them tell a little bit about themselves, and then I tell them about stealing the quarter. I focus not only on how good I felt after confessing my misdeed, but also on how good my mother felt. She felt good because someone she loved dearly had learned from his mistake and wanted to get back on the right path. Then I open my Bible and read Jesus' story of the shepherd and the lost sheep. When the shepherd learns that one of his flock of a hundred has strayed and gotten lost, he leaves the ninety-nine and goes off in search of the wayward sheep. When he finds it, he returns home and invites his family and neighbors to come together to rejoice with him. Jesus concludes the story with these words, "I tell you, in just the same way there will be more joy in heaven over one sinner who repents than over ninety-nine righteous people who have no need of repentance" (Luke 15:7).

Knowing that God is pleased and joyful about their desire to overcome their sins gives children a great deal of incentive to live good and decent lives. The same is true for the rest of us. Jesus' message was one of redemption and the goodness of humankind. His words and his life have brought healing to so many who were burdened with the weight of their mistakes—including me.

The prophet Isaiah captured Jesus' role among us so well: "The people who walked in darkness have seen a great light; upon those who dwelt in the land of gloom a light has shone" (Isaiah 9:1). Darkness is not forever.

CHAPTER THIRTEEN

God Doesn't Own a Trash Barrel

There's a wonderful story behind one of the world's best-known and best-loved works of art, the statue of David by the great sixteenth century Italian artist Buonarroti Michelangelo.

The block of marble Michelangelo used for his magnificent David was originally delivered to the studio of another Florentine artist. That sculptor examined the marble very carefully, found flaws and imperfections, and rejected it as unusable. Because they didn't want to waste their trip or lose out on a sale, the quarrymen took the same block of marble to Michelangelo's studio to see if he might want it.

Michelangelo, too, examined the marble very carefully and noticed its flaws and imperfections. But instead of rejecting it, he saw the block of flawed marble as a challenge to his genius and skill as an artist. He purchased it, and from that imperfect stone sculpted one of the most prized pieces of art in the world.[4]

This story may be apocryphal, like the stories of many distant historical figures. But true or not, it serves as a wonderful allegory for the way humans and God view human life.

Like the sculptor who rejected the block of marble, some people quickly reject and discard others simply because those others are different, with the view that "different" means flawed and imperfect. Such thinking leads to the attitude and judgment that some human lives are more valuable than others.

We witnessed this moral cancer during World War II, when millions of Jews were exterminated by the Nazi evil. We witnessed it, to our own shame in America, when we allowed the practice of slavery. It also appears in our past treatment of and attitude toward people with disabilities. President Franklin Roosevelt would never appear in public in a wheelchair, some say because he was afraid the American public would lack confidence in a president who was crippled by polio.

God is the sculptor of each of our lives. He sees our flaws and imperfections, but like Michelangelo, he also sees the potential each of us has for greatness and beauty. God simply doesn't make mistakes. There's not a trash barrel anywhere near him.

Watching the way some people dismiss and dispose of the lives of the "flawed and imperfect" must bring great sadness to heaven. But it also prompted God to spring into action, sending Jesus into our world to heal it of this horrible cancer. At the heart of Jesus' teachings and example lies the dignity, sacredness, and equality of all human beings. While he lived on the earth he engaged and reached out to women, Gentiles, Samaritans, lepers, Romans, public sinners, and all those who had been rejected or treated as inferior by his fellow Jews. He was roundly criticized for his example of inclusion, but he didn't hesitate to challenge the hypocrisy and evil he saw around him.

In the thirteenth chapter of Luke's Gospel, Jesus tells a story that reminds me of the story of Michelangelo and the statue of David. A landowner is out inspecting the fig trees on his property. He notices a particular fig tree that has failed to produce any figs. Unhappy with its lack of production, he orders his farm manager to rip it out of the ground and burn it.

This was a common practice in Palestine, where fig trees were plentiful and easy to grow. If one tree failed to produce, the farmer destroyed it and replaced it with a new tree. But Jesus' story ends differently. The farm manager pleads with the impatient owner to give the fig tree a second chance. "Let me work with the fig tree for a year," the manager says, "and if by next harvest it still isn't producing figs, then we can cut it down and burn it."

People who dismiss or dispose of people whom they judge to be flawed or imperfect are like the impatient landowner. The farm manager who pleads to be given a chance to work with the nonproducing fig tree is a Christ figure. Jesus makes it clear that God believes in us and has sent Jesus into the world to work with us so that our lives will produce a bountiful harvest of love and service.

A few years back, a man fired a gun from his car at a boy whom he believed had disrespected him in some way. The man was tried and convicted of his crime, and at his sentencing, the mother of the young victim was allowed to address him. Her words were televised on the evening newscast: "Sir, I would like to know at what precise point in your life you came to the conclusion that God no longer believed in you and loved you? I want to know because at that moment, you must have also stopped believing in and loving yourself."

That grieving mother couldn't have captured what had gone wrong in that man's life any more eloquently. If we believe that God has given up on us, if we believe that God no longer cares what we do with our lives, then we no longer care about our own life. We no longer believe in the value of others.

Remembering and embracing God's view of humankind—the sacredness, dignity, and equality of every person—is a constant challenge. When somebody cuts in front of me in the supermarket checkout line, I'm tempted to think that God doesn't value and love that person. God couldn't possibly care about people who have no business parking in handicap-access spaces but do it anyway. And yes, there are times when I wonder how God can possibly love and value me.

But where we see weakness, God sees the possibility for greatness. I remember reading somewhere a story about a missionary priest, assigned to a Pacific island with very few trees, whose first task was to build a church for worship. He used the only materials available, the flotsam and jetsam that had washed up on the shore. Out of packing boxes, driftwood, and other debris, the priest built a serviceable chapel. As I read that story, I couldn't help but think of how Jesus did the same thing in building his church. He constructed it out of sinners as well as saints, the weak as well as the strong.

When I'm tempted to doubt my value, I remember Jesus' words: "Are not five sparrows sold for two small coins? Yet not one of them has escaped the notice of God. Even the hairs of your head have all been counted. Do not be afraid. You are worth more than many sparrows" (Luke 12:6-7). Each of our lives has a purpose and a place known to God. In his sight, every one of us is valuable.

CHAPTER FOURTEEN

The Patience of God

In the old days of Sunday worship in the Catholic church, the priest used to celebrate the Mass with his back to the congregation as he faced the crucifix on the wall. Then in the 1960s, when Catholic worship and liturgy went through extensive reforms, the priest began praying the Mass facing the people.

This may seem a small thing, but many of us priests found this change difficult. Facing the folks in the pews for a good hour was a major source of distraction. We could see everything that was going on, from parents scolding their children to the head usher sneaking out to have a cigarette. Trying to focus our thoughts and energy on the words and symbols of this sacred time of sacrament and prayer challenged priests like me whose minds easily wander.

But what most threatens my concentration at Sunday Mass is not those who come late or depart early, nor those who take an intermission for a bathroom or a cigarette break, nor the brothers and sisters who continue the teasing and rib poking they began before they left home. The sneezes, the hacks, the coughs, and the occasional burps don't faze me one little bit. There's only one thing that unravels my concentration and disconnects me from the presence of God, just as surely as pulling the electrical plug on a television disconnects me from the evening news: the sound of a crying child.

I'm not talking about a soft whimper or an occasional cry that dies almost as swiftly as it began. I'm talking about industrial strength crying, the kind that is unrelenting, shrill, bone piercing in its intensity, painful to the ear. When a child cries at this level, I think even God steps outside of the church for a break.

On one memorable Sunday, I was just starting my sermon at the eleven o'clock Mass. Somewhere from the middle pews, a child began to cry. It started slowly and hesitantly, like the beginning of a fire engine siren, but I knew a full-throated wail was to follow.

As the wail grew in volume, I tried to compensate both by speaking louder and by bringing the microphone closer to my mouth. Nothing worked. The baby's cry drowned out every attempt to talk over him and shattered the flow of my thoughts and the rhythm of my delivery. The parents' attempts to quiet their child were sincere, but futile.

At one point as I stumbled through my sermon, they gave the baby their car keys to play with. This only made matters worse as the child repeatedly dropped the set of keys on the wooden pew seat. Now we had the child's wail and the loud clatter of the keys echoing off the pew. I knew it was hopeless to continue, so I wished my parishioners the blessings of the day and returned to the altar to continue the Mass.

Not once did I look, let alone glare, at the parents or their child. I would never knowingly do anything to cause embarrassment to another. But I must confess that my thoughts were less than Christlike. I prayed the parents would take their child outside, or even that the baby would have a small medical emergency and need short-term care. As Mass continued, so did my irritation. The baby didn't let up for a moment. If anything, he got louder.

Finally, the time came for the congregation to come forward to receive Holy Communion, the holiest and most sacred moment of Mass. In my parish, as in many parishes, the custom is for the parents to bring their children with them so the priest can give the little ones a blessing even though they are not yet old enough for Communion.

I hoped and prayed the crying child and his parents would not choose my communion line. I just didn't want to bless the little son of God who had been such a source of disruption that morning. Maybe if he were standing in the exorcism line, I would have felt different. But in my pettiness, my smallness, I didn't want to bless him.

My prayer that the parents would choose the other communion line was one of those that God said no to. As the family drew near, I noticed the child was wearing a little sweatshirt that had some kind of message on it. When the parents presented him for the blessing, my eyes went to the message on his chest: "Be patient with me; God is not finished yet."

It was an epiphany moment for me, a much-needed awakening. God's act of creation is an *ongoing* action. God is never finished creating, and nowhere is this truer than in his human creations. Whether a baby in our parents' arms, a recent college graduate, or a senior citizen, God isn't finished with us yet.

For Christians, our goal this side of heaven is to develop into Christlike men and women. God was still in the early stages of crafting that little child's life into a Christ figure. Neither the child nor his parents needed to make any apology for his behavior in church that morning. God had taken a heck of a lot more time to work with me and craft my life into a Christ figure, and given my pettiness and irritation toward the child, he probably had more work left to do with me than he did with that child!

The good news of Jesus is that God never gives up on us. It just takes him longer to create some of us than others. Be patient. God is not finished yet!

CHAPTER FIFTEEN

The Cross: God's Pledge

On Valentine's Day many Catholic parishes celebrate a special Mass for married couples. This is a wonderful opportunity for spouses to come together, often with their children, and renew their marriage vows before God in their church. As a celibate priest, I don't know a great deal about marriage, but I do know that it needs to be celebrated and affirmed.

One year, as Valentine's Day neared, the folks in my parish decided to ask all the couples who were going to attend the special Mass to bring with them a special symbol that silently spoke of their love and commitment. They were also invited, if they were comfortable, to stand up during the designated time in the service and share the meaning and the message behind that cherished symbol.

The stories and sharing that night were many and moving. One couple displayed their wedding rings, which had been the wedding rings of their grandparents. The rings had been melted down and remade into new rings, joining two generations. Another couple proudly presented their three little children. As the father balanced two of them in his arms, he spoke of them as living symbols of the love and commitment he shared with his wife. Arrayed and shared that night were candles, house keys, poems, letters, photographs, and a host of other special symbols.

But the symbol shared by a couple who had been married just a year or two short of fifty years stood out from the rest.

Harold and Margaret shyly stood in front of us as they unwrapped a couple of layers of tinfoil and displayed a delicious-looking peach pie. They explained that, like most couples, they had had their disagreements. Sometimes these would boil over into heated exchanges in which things were said and incidents from the past brought up that left them both feeling hurt and wounded. After the exchange, they would go off alone to lick their wounds. Some days, Harold just left for work; other times, they retreated to separate parts of the house.

Margaret said that during this time in the desert, she always went through two emotions. The first was an intense weariness with Harold. His stubbornness, pride, and need to always be right was wearing on her, testing her, tiring her. Her sense of weariness would quickly run its course, however, and be replaced by a much more powerful emotion. She loved Harold, loved him deeply.

Early in their marriage, Margaret searched for a way to reach out and reconcile with Harold after an argument, something to break the silence between them. It didn't take her long to settle on peach pie. It was Harold's favorite dessert, reserved for those special celebrations in their family life. Peach pie was often the centerpiece of birthday, Thanksgiving, and Fourth of July gatherings. For Margaret to make peach pie meant extra effort, extra love.

So Margaret chose peach pie as a symbol of her love for Harold in those times when their love was tested. When that peach pie was in the oven, the smells of cinnamon, sugar, and peaches drifted through the house, piercing even the wall of silence that separated her and Harold.

The Cross: God's Pledge

When the aroma reached Harold, he didn't think about the peach pie. He thought about the woman who was baking it, his wife, the most important person in his life. She was the one who loved him, believed in him, and gave him strength. When the aroma reached Margaret, she didn't think about the peach pie. She thought about the man that she had baked it for, her husband, the most important person in her life.

The peach pie was home to Harold and Margaret's love story. It was their way of saying that they had not given up on each other. Their love was too strong, and the alternative to forgiving each other and going on was unthinkable. When they unwrapped the pie and explained its significance that night in church, their fellow parishioners responded with a long, thoughtful silence and then a round of applause.

When I remember Harold and Margaret's story, I think of the cross of Jesus, arguably the single most readily identifiable symbol in the world today. People look at a cross and know immediately the story behind it, just as the people who had been in church that Valentine's night know the story behind Margaret and Harold's peach pie. The cross of Jesus symbolizes the love story between God and each one of us. It speaks of both the rift and the reconciliation between us, just as surely as the peach pie spoke of Harold and Margaret's rift and reconciliation.

We read often in our Christian Scriptures that God grows weary with our stubbornness, pride, and failure to live up to the covenant we made with him through Moses, Abraham, and the prophets. God's patience with us is often tested—but it has never been broken. "For they broke my covenant and I grew weary of them, says the Lord. But ... I will be their God, and they shall be my people," he says to us in Hebrews 8:9-10.

The cross of Jesus is THE symbol of God's saving action in our lives. It is the definitive pledge that God has not and will not give up on any of us. At times I wonder how God can possibly love me and want to share eternity with the likes of me. But then I look at the cross, remember its story, and am once again drawn to him.

SECTION FOUR

"Hey, Father!
Does God Really Expect Me to Forgive?"

CHAPTER SIXTEEN

There Is No Peace Without Forgiveness

The absence of laughter, the grim faces, the tears and tight voices all signaled that something was very wrong with this group of high school sophomores. Their eyes drooped from lack of sleep, their bodies slumped from fatigue, and their hands trembled out of fear and shock. What brought us together was a planning meeting for a memorial service. Their friend and classmate Katy, along with her mother, had been brutally murdered.

This memorial service was critical for our school community for two reasons. One, it gave us the opportunity to pray for the dead. Our scriptures (see 2 Maccabees 12:44-46) tell us that it is a good and holy thing to pray for those who have died. Two, and even more importantly, we needed a time of prayer for ourselves, a special time to aid the healing of hearts that had been badly wounded and lives that had been badly shaken.

Only one medication can ease the hurt that the death of a sixteen-year-old girl and her mother brings: our shared Christian faith in resurrection. It is the only light and hope in the midst of this seemingly impenetrable darkness. The young sophomores gathered for our meeting had before them the task of bringing the healing message of our faith into a grieving community.

At the meeting's end, everyone seemed pleased with the results of our planning. But I was troubled. A piece was missing.

I hesitated to bring it up, unsure of the welcome it would receive, but I knew that I must voice my thoughts. Taking a deep breath, I plunged ahead: "I couldn't help but notice that there is no mention in our service of the man who murdered Katy. He certainly is in need of our prayers at this time. More importantly, we need to pray for the strength and faith to forgive him for what he has done. We can't hate. It will poison us."

My words were unwelcome and disturbing. I could feel the anger. A pressure, like the gases inside a volcano, began to build in the room, and I sensed that an explosion was coming. It didn't take long. One of the boys who had been especially close to Katy, his face red with fury, got to his feet and with a trembling finger pointed in my direction. "Hey, Father!" he hissed. "You can't make us forgive that S.O.B." Equally upset was the girl sitting next to him, who said to me in a choked voice, "You put that prayer in the service and I'll walk out."

They were not alone in their feelings. The rest of the group shared their views with the same intensity and passion. How could they possibly forgive someone so evil that he had murdered their friend and classmate? How could they forgive someone whose cruelty brought them such grief and pain? These young folks were telling me, "Father, you're asking for more than we can possibly give."

Maybe I was; maybe it was too soon and maybe they were too young and vulnerable. But in the deepest part of my heart, I don't think I was wrong to ask this of them. The very same Christian faith that we turn to for comfort, hope, and meaning in the face of death and suffering demands a great deal of us in return, including forgiveness of those who harm us. Isn't that exactly what we repeatedly pray for in the Lord's Prayer? "Forgive us our trespasses as we forgive those who trespass against us." God asks not for token words of forgiveness, but for genuine, authentic forgiveness of those who have brought us harm. Difficult as it is, forgiveness of our enemies is central to the Christian life.

In parables, in straight talk, and in the drama of his own life, Jesus demanded that we forgive with the same generous spirit with which God forgives us. Remember Jesus' parable of the unforgiving servant in Matthew 18:21-35? A king generously forgave the debt of his servant because the man had no means to repay his debt. The forgiven debtor then went out and refused to do the same thing for his fellow servant who owed him money. When the king heard about his servant's unforgiving behavior, he had him thrown into jail. Jesus concludes that story with these words in verse 35: "So will my heavenly Father do to you, unless each of you forgives his brother from his heart."

It wasn't just in stories that Jesus preached the message of forgiveness. His own life witnessed to a generous and, at times, heroic forgiveness of those who harmed him. Certainly his most memorable witness to the power of forgiveness was on the cross. His enemies had done everything in their power to discredit him. Now they were about to take his life. They had no remorse, no contrition for what they had done to him. Yet, incredibly, in the last moments of his life, Jesus summoned up enough strength to pray, "Father, forgive them, they know not what they do" (Luke 23:34).

The heart of Jesus is forgiveness. Yet we, his disciples, often withhold it. When someone hurts us or someone we love, we don't want to forgive them. We're angry, and our anger shuts out this part of Jesus' message. We wrestle with the injustice and unfairness of the wrong we have received. Sometimes not even contrition and restitution is sufficient for us. We want more, sometimes even revenge. Our anger and resentment poison us, affecting the health of every part of our life. Forgiveness, as Jesus so freely and generously gave it, is so very, very difficult for us—even for priests.

When I challenged the sophomores to include prayers of forgiveness for Katy's killer in the memorial service, I must confess that I was thinking more of what this would mean in their lives than I was in the life of the murderer. They couldn't carry their hate and anger with them or they would be the ones to suffer, not the killer. When they replied angrily to my challenge that they would never forgive that man and they would walk out if we included prayers for him, I backed off.

I relented because I was genuinely afraid of a scene at the memorial service. Demanding of them something they weren't ready to give would have backed them into a corner, and their reaction would have divided our community, not united it. But I also relented because I know that forgiveness is a process. We often need to go through stages of anger, resentment, and pain before healing can begin—healing that will eventually make authentic forgiveness something we are capable of. The process takes time, especially for the young, who are still novices in dealing with their feelings and con-flicting emotions.

Looking back, I am not sure I made the right choice in back-ing off. How could those teenagers know and experience for themselves the grace and blessing that the act of forgiveness brings to wounded spirits unless they were challenged to do so? How could they know the peace that releasing anger and resentment brings unless they did so? Forgiveness is as much for us and our own spiritual health as it is for the one forgiven.

The memorial service was emotional. It's just plain hard to watch young people you care about struggling so painfully with their grief. But it was also a beginning to the healing process. On a bulletin board over my desk, I've pinned a newspaper photograph taken during the service, which took place in the high school gym. It shows Katy's classmates seated in the bleachers with their arms wrapped around one another, seeking comfort by resting their heads on the shoulder of the one next to them, their bodies intertwined.

That extraordinary photograph reminds me of something I once read about the redwood trees of Northern California. Although among the tallest trees in the world, the redwoods have a very shallow root system. What gives them their strength, what enables them to withstand strong winds without toppling over, is the fact that they grow in groves and their roots are intertwined with one another. Our students got through this storm by drawing their strength from one another.

That newspaper photograph is yellow with age now. When I look at it today, I sometimes think about Katy's killer, who is serving a life sentence in prison. I also think about her friends and classmates. I wonder how they would respond now, some twenty years after that terrible tragedy, if we had another memorial service and I asked them to include a prayer of forgiveness for her murderer. Something tells me time has allowed the process of forgiveness to run its course. At least, that has been my prayer.

CHAPTER SEVENTEEN

Struggling to Forgive

I have served under four archbishops during my ministry as a priest. I've admired and respected all four as genuinely Christ-like men and leaders, although they have been very different in style and personality. I confess to having a favorite among the four, however, and that was Archbishop Thomas Murphy, who led the Archdiocese of Seattle until his untimely death of leukemia in 1997, after serving a mere six years as our archbishop.

Archbishop Murphy was an Irish Catholic from Chicago who was warm and outgoing and had a knack for making you feel like you were his confidant and closest friend. He cared little for the pomp and pageantry that surrounds some of our church's hierarchy and was as down-to-earth as one could possibly be. I loved his self-effacing manner and genuine humanness.

Just before Archbishop Murphy's death, a local television station sent a reporter to his home to do a story about him. In the course of the interview, the Archbishop alluded to his Irish temperament. The reporter asked him if he could describe exactly what the Irish temperament was. Archbishop Murphy paused thoughtfully for a moment or two and said, "The best way I can describe it is with a story."

Before he was appointed an archbishop, he went on, he was serving as a pastor in a Chicago parish. He became very sick with a life-threatening illness and had to be hospitalized. Once the danger was over, he said, he remembered everyone who came to visit him during his time in the hospital. Then, with a slight smile on his face and mischief in his eyes, he added, "I also remembered everyone who didn't."

His honesty about his own humanness, even when it revealed his flaws and smallness at times, drew people to Archbishop Murphy. He wasn't afraid to say that even archbishops have trouble living up to the daily demands of the gospel of Jesus. They are just as subject to fail at forgiveness, to harbor resentments, and to carry grudges as the next person. Being an archbishop doesn't grant immunity from sin.

What's true of archbishops is even truer of priests like me. I preach forgiveness, I teach forgiveness, I counsel forgiveness—and at times I struggle with offering forgiveness. One incident in particular stands out for me. For years, I kept two goldfish in a small glass bowl that rested on a ledge next to my desk in my classroom. I wasn't nearly as attached to the fish as I am to my dogs, but I took good care of them. For some reason, though, they never seemed to live very long. I suspect my students used to feed them bits of chocolate and potato chips, hastening them to their graves year after year.

One morning I walked into my third period class, a group that had more than its quota of mischievous students, and saw a couple of boys wrestling near the goldfish. One of them, Kevin, accidentally knocked the goldfish bowl off the ledge. It shattered on the floor, dumping the water, and leaving the poor fish flopping about in a desperate struggle for life. One of the students grabbed a wastebasket, raced down the hall to the bathroom, filled it with water and came running back to the room. But it was too late; the goldfish were dead.

I could feel my anger building, and I prayed for the strength to keep my mouth shut for fear I would say something I would regret. Kevin tried to apologize, but I would have none of it. I had no thoughts of forgiveness, just dark thoughts of Kevin hanging by his thumbs. With my best withering stare, I sent him to his seat and began the day's lesson.

The centerpiece of the class that day was a twenty-minute movie about a future society that had outlawed all religions from its midst. The government had forbidden all religious teachings, worship, literature, and church buildings. With the goldfish still very much on my mind, I opened the class discussion with the question, "Can anybody tell me what values religion brings to a society?"

Not one hand went up. The whole class knew I was still steaming over the goldfish. Their silence and unresponsiveness threw oil on my fire, and I repeated in an icy voice, "You mean there's not one of you who can tell me what values religion adds to society? Come on, just give me one value. Somebody! Anybody!"

Slowly, timidly, Kevin raised his hand. At first I ignored it— that hand that had the blood of my goldfish on it. The seconds ticked by in silence. No one else raised a hand. With clenched teeth, I said, "All right, Kevin, give me one value that religious faith brings to our lives." In a halting, nervous voice, Kevin said, "Forgiveness, Father?"

His words stuck a needle in the balloon of my anger, releasing it instantly. I knew he spoke the truth, and I felt like the fool I was. It was an epiphany moment.

None of us can love well, serve well, pray well, or teach well if we harbor resentment. Anger and resentment block the flow of the fruits of God's Spirit, damming them as surely as the wooden bulwarks of the beaver. The inability to forgive has caused wars between countries, divorce in families, the breakup of long friendships, the destruction of careers, and the bankruptcy of our spirituality. A hardened heart is a useless heart. If we can't forgive others or experience their forgiveness, we drag a weight behind us that drains our energy and our progress in life.

As a teacher and priest who should know all this, I digested Kevin's words and realized that my failure to forgive had created a barrier between the class and myself. My unwillingness to forgive was a poison that had claimed many victims.

As Kevin's words, "Forgiveness, Father?" hung in the air, thirty other teenagers fixed their eyes on me as they waited for my response. Students are particularly sensitive about whether there is consistency between what we adults say and what we do. Their priests perhaps receive even more scrutiny than their parents and teachers. Young people can live with our flaws—if we openly acknowledge them and assure them we're trying to do better.

I knew that now was a time for honesty or it was going to be a long year in that classroom. So, humbled and embarrassed by my own failure to model what I taught, I said, "I'm really sorry for my anger. I know it was an accident."

There was a long silence, and then one of the boys said, "Hey, Father! It's OK. We've all had bad days."

Not exactly the words of forgiveness that I offer penitents in the sacrament of confession, but they had the same effect.

Kevin approached me after class. "I'm really sorry about your goldfish, Father. I'll bring some new ones in tomorrow," he said. Then he added thoughtfully, "I think I learned something today about forgiveness."

I think he had. And I had, too.

CHAPTER EIGHTEEN

Meaning What You Say

She sat in my school office with tears streaming down her face. "Father, Ben and I are getting a divorce." Jennifer's words caught me off guard, especially considering what had passed between us just a few months before.

Some ten years earlier, I had officiated at Ben and Jennifer's wedding. A few months ago, the couple had called and asked if they could come by to talk. As soon as they walked in the door I knew something was terribly wrong between them. They ignored the couch and sat in chairs on opposite sides of the room. Ben kept his head down and wouldn't look at either of us, and Jennifer's eyes were red and her make-up streaked.

In a halting voice, Jennifer told a painful tale of Ben's infidelity, an affair with a coworker. She was devastated. Ben said that he felt terrible about what he had done. They said they loved each other and wanted to make their marriage work; they planned to begin marriage counseling. They had come to my office because they wanted to involve God in their new start with each other. They asked me to bless Jennifer's gift of forgiveness to Ben and to witness a renewal of their marriage vows.

We went into the school chapel next door, and in that sacred space I offered a prayer of thanksgiving for their reconciliation, for Jennifer's gift of forgiveness, and for Ben's contrition and desire to make amends. Then, holding hands and locking their eyes together, the couple slowly repeated their marriage vows of ten years before. It was a powerful moment, a moment in which I felt God's grace at work.

The clear memory of that afternoon prompted my surprise when Jennifer told me only a few months later that she and Ben were divorcing. What had happened?

"I can't forgive him, Father," she told me. She had mouthed the words of forgiveness to Ben, but she hadn't forgiven him. She wasn't able to let go of her anger and resentment over his betrayal. She put them away, out of sight, but she could retrieve them any time. When they had a disagreement, she pulled them out and used them against him. Her anger and resentment still lay just below the surface. Like a wedge, her lack of forgiveness drove them further and further apart.

When we genuinely forgive another, we wrap our words around love and trust. We release our anger and resentment. They're gone, never to be retrieved, never to be revisited. This is the kind of forgiveness God offers to us and asks that we offer to one another.

There's a wonderful story about a nun who, much to her dismay, had frequent visions at night. In these visions, God would appear and offer her words of encouragement in her vocation. She didn't know if the visions were real or whether they were hallucinations. Disturbed, she finally went to the bishop, told him what was happening, and asked him what he thought was going on.

The bishop was extremely skeptical. "I know of one sure way to tell if these visions are authentic," he said. "The next time God appears to you, ask him what my greatest sin was. If your visitor knows that, then it really is God appearing to you."

A few days later, the good nun returned to the bishop with

the news that God had appeared to her again. "And did you ask God what my greatest sin was?" asked the bishop.

"I did," the nun replied. "And God said, 'I don't remember.'"[5]

Once God forgives, God forgets—and we are to do the same. Can you imagine going to heaven and having God say, every time your paths crossed, "Just remember, you made it up here by the skin of your teeth. I remember that affair you had, and I'm keeping an eye on you."

In St. John's Gospel, chapter 20, verse 23, Jesus confers upon the twelve apostles the power to forgive sins. He says to them, "Whose sins you forgive are forgiven them, and whose sins you retain are retained." If you go back to the original Greek, the verb "forgive" is *aphienai* and means not only to forgive, but also to release from one's grasp. The verb "retain" is from the Greek verb *kratein*, which means to retain within one's grasp, hence to deny forgiveness.

Forgiveness is difficult. In fact, it's one of the most difficult things God asks of us. As a Catholic priest, I'm very much in the "forgiveness business." I've spent thousands of hours in the confessional and at reconciliation services. I know firsthand the power of God's forgiveness in people's lives, how it turns them from destructive paths.

And as one who has sinned and has offended God and neighbor, I know the grace of forgiveness in my own life. Countless times, genuine forgiveness has given me a fresh start with my God and with others. Knowing that my sins are forgotten, that my past is not carried with me, makes all the difference. When God forgives, he means what he says.

CHAPTER NINETEEN

Once Is Not Enough

One morning, just before the school bell announced the beginning of first period, the frightening sound of two cars colliding at the busy intersection outside the main entrance jolted me from my thoughts about the day ahead.

Whenever there is an accident near the school, my heart races; the odds are pretty good that one of our students is involved. I hurried outside to see how I could help, and sure enough, one of the cars was a student's.

Physically, both drivers were fine, but Stephanie wasn't doing well emotionally. She sat in the driver's seat of her car, shaken and very frightened, her hands still tightly gripping the steering wheel. When I asked her if she was hurt, she just kept repeating over and over again, "My father is going to kill me! My father is going to kill me!" When I assured her that her father was going to do no such thing, she said, "You don't understand. This is my third accident. He's going to kill me!"

The police came, the cars were towed away, and we finally got Stephanie settled down in the nurse's office while we called her father to tell him what had happened. He asked to talk to his daughter. She took the phone, and I could see her face tighten as she prepared to receive news of her imminent death.

Father and daughter talked quietly for a few minutes. When Stephanie hung up the phone, she didn't look any less agitated. "He was only being nice because you're here, Father," she said.

In Stephanie's mind, in that youthful tendency to overdramatize, the end of the world was just hours away, when she would see her father in person.

Instead, Stephanie learned a very valuable lesson. When I ran into her at school the next day and asked her how things had gone at home, she beamed and said, "Dad was great! He was worried about *me*, not the stupid car." Rather than bringing out her father's wrath, the accident had resulted in a wonderful, loving moment between them, giving her father the perfect opportunity to reassure Stephanie that she was the most important treasure in his life. Stephanie glowed as she told me about it.

Stephanie had been so upset because she was worried about how her father would react to her third accident in a year. After each of the previous two, she had promised to be more careful in the future. Each time he had renewed his trust in her. Was there a limit to his patience? How many times could he forgive? Her father's response taught her that when you truly love someone, your forgiveness is generous and limitless.

I don't know whether Stephanie's father learned limitless forgiveness from Jesus or whether it sprang from the instincts of his heart. But Jesus challenged his followers to extend this gift to one another whenever it was asked for. In the Gospel of St. Matthew we read, "Then Peter approaching asked him, 'Lord, if my brother sins against me, how often must I forgive him? As many as seven times?' Jesus answered, 'I say to you, not seven times but seventy-seven times'" (Matthew 18:21-22). In other words, we are to forgive as many times as forgiveness is needed.

I have never understood the mentality behind the "three strikes and you're out" law that has been legislated by some of our states in this country. Those found guilty of three felonies are sentenced to life behind bars without the possibility of parole. This seems so at odds with both our Christian belief in human redemption and our call not to put limits on our forgiveness.

I like to tell a certain story at penance and reconciliation services with our young people. The incident took place at a time when punishments for crime were very harsh and cruel. A man had been convicted of stealing sheep. As punishment, the authorities branded the letters "ST" on his forehead, announcing to the village that he was a sheep thief. As the years went by, the man made amends for his dishonesty by a life spent in generous service of others. The villagers forgave and forgot his crime, for he had won their respect and admiration. In the twilight of his life, a mother and her young child struck up a conversation with him at the village market. Afterward, the child asked his mother about the "ST" still prominent on his forehead. "Oh," the mother said, "those letters stand for saint."[6]

Whether we are a sheep thief, a three-times-convicted criminal, or a three-time fender bender like Stephanie, unconditional, limitless forgiveness empowers us to move forward without the burden of our past mistakes. Knowing that others believe in our goodness enables us to live good and decent lives. God has done this for us and expects us to do this for one another.

Of course, it's easier to offer limitless forgiveness to those we love. It's a challenge to offer it to the stranger. This is particularly true for me when I drive my car. Rude drivers, inattentive drivers, law-flaunting drivers—they all tax my limits. That's why I have scotch-taped Jesus' words from Matthew to the center post of my steering wheel: "Not seven times, but seventy-seven times." It helps.

CHAPTER TWENTY

Forgive and Live Longer

Maybe Jesus insisted time and time again that we forgive those who trespass against us because it's good for our health. At least that's what some of the early returns of research into the effects of forgiveness indicate.

According to an article that appeared in the July 4, 1999, edition of the *Seattle Times*, research from the University of Wisconsin in Madison reveals that anger and the unwillingness to forgive can damage the health of the body. Although the research was not completed at the time, preliminary results of the study indicated that the less people forgave, the more diseases they had and the more medical symptoms they reported. Conversely, researchers strongly suspected that the act of forgiving could actually improve a person's well-being.

The same article, written by reporter Julie Sevrens of Knight Ridder Newspapers, touches on similar work going on at Stanford University, which is host to a program called the Stanford Forgiveness Project. Theorizing that the act of forgiveness can benefit both individuals and society at large, scientists have launched research that has begun to demonstrate that forgiveness can positively enhance emotional and, quite possibly, physical health. Studies about the physical benefits of forgiveness are too limited for anyone to make sweeping generalizations, but the positive psychological benefits—including less stress, anxiety, and depression—have been widely reported by researchers.

Obviously, research on forgiveness is still in its early stages, but early results confirm what many of us know in our hearts. When we can't bring ourselves to forgive, we carry with us feelings of anger, resentment, and hostility that irritate us like a rash that won't go away. Even if we can put these disturbing feelings out of our minds for a time, inevitably they break out anew. They cause insomnia, affect our work, and intrude on our happiness. A smoldering grudge lies in the pit of our stomach like a foreign object that cries to be removed. We don't need conclusive research to tell us that the inability to forgive threatens us spiritually and physically.

Often we read in the newspapers about another incident of road rage. One motorist fails to signal, cuts someone off in traffic, or commits some other driving sin. Rather than simply forgive, forget, and go on with his or her day, the offended driver becomes consumed with rage and the need to retaliate. All common sense flies out the window. The drivers throw heated, angry words back and forth. Threatening gestures and menacing movements signal the beginning of physical confrontation.

We read these horrible stories in the comfort of our homes and wonder why these folks can't simply let their anger go. Is it worth jeopardizing your life, your family, your career, and even your freedom? When I read stories about road rage, I scratch my head at the foolishness of allowing someone you don't even know to threaten your life span.

I think Jesus made forgiveness a centerpiece of Christian faith not because he was concerned about our physical health, but because it is so critical to the health of our spirit. It's hard to pray when we are angry. It's hard to be humble and gentle when pride consumes and directs our lives. It's almost impossible to find joy and peace when our souls are crowded with anger and resentment. It's hard to be concerned about the welfare of others when we have excluded certain people from our compassion and love. Such is the high price of unforgiveness.

On the other hand, forgiveness has many rewards. It blesses and graces both the one forgiven and the one forgiving. It defuses the destructiveness of revenge, scatters the building storm of anger, and expels the demons that would take over our lives in the mad pursuit to right a perceived wrong. Forgiveness replaces these evil passions with an inner calm and tranquility of the soul. At least this is what forgiveness has done in my own life.

One December, a week before Christmas, I was in our chapel with two freshman classes celebrating our church's sacrament of reconciliation and penance. It was the last of eighteen straight such services held over a three-day period, and I was tired.

About five minutes into the service, two of the freshman girls in a back pew began an animated conversation. Their behavior distracted those around them and irritated me. I stopped the service, and in the silence that followed, I gave these two young ladies my most intimidating and withering stare. This tactic normally works on freshmen, but not this time. Little Sarah kept it up and my Irish temper got the best of me. I made her stand up, and then proceeded to publicly, and with unnecessary sarcasm, chew her out. True, she deserved to be corrected, but she didn't deserve my sarcasm or the humiliation that followed my words.

As I resumed the service of the Lord's forgiveness, I felt

horrible. I could see the pain of humiliation in Sarah's tears and red face. I could have handled the situation so much better, and I deserved the guilt I felt. I didn't feel good, and I had brought my illness upon myself.

At the end of the service I asked each of the students, as their penance, to pray three "Our Fathers" for three different people that they had hurt in recent days. Then the bell rang and the students began to file quietly out of the chapel. One student remained behind. In the darkness, broken only by the candles flickering on the Advent wreath, I saw little Sarah. In a hesitant, tearful voice, she said, "Father, I'm sorry for upsetting you. I just wanted to tell you that I prayed each of those 'Our Fathers' for you."

I desperately needed those words at that moment. My guilt at the way I had treated Sarah was not something I wanted to take home with me. Her words started the healing within me, but I needed to take the next step. I put my arm around her and said, "No, Sarah. I need to ask your forgiveness for the way I treated you. I have more to be sorry about than you. Please forgive me."

Sarah and I left the chapel that afternoon together, each of us feeling good inside. We felt no anger, no resentment, no stewing over what had happened between us. She and I remained good friends over the years, and she honored me by asking me to witness her wedding twelve years later. It was an honor that never would have been possible if we hadn't given the gift of forgiveness to each other before we left the chapel that day.

I'm also convinced that I am going to live a tad longer simply because Sarah and I forgave each other that day.

SECTION FIVE

"Hey, Father!
Where Is God When Bad Things Happen?"

CHAPTER TWENTY-ONE

Rebuilding After the Fire

When I drove up to the house, I saw yellow police tape circling the yard, keeping the curious at bay. White smoke drifted up from what had been the kitchen and family room. I ducked under the tape and found Bill and Sandra standing in their driveway, arm in arm, surveying what was left of their possessions—barely recognizable globs of melted metal, broken ceramics, scorched picture frames, and blackened furniture and appliances.

The fire had broken out in the early morning hours, and by the time Bill and Sandra had been alerted by its sound and smell, they had barely enough time to wake their son and daughters and flee. They were helpless to do anything but watch the relentless flames consume their home and its contents.

I had come as their pastor, but Bill and Sandra got the first words out. "Father, we're all OK. We all got out. That's all that matters." No one had died, no one had been hurt. It was only "stuff" that was snatched away from them, "stuff" that could easily be replaced.

But I knew they had a difficult challenge ahead of them. They had not only a house to rebuild, but their confidence, hope, and trust in their world. That task would be much more daunting than replacing the house and the clothing, utensils, and furniture that had burned with it. A fire that destroys a home hits at a very personal level. It violates its victims and invades their lives. Bill, Sandra, and their children were all disturbed by thoughts of what might have happened if they hadn't gotten out in time. Memories of their close call would continue to intrude on their sleep, their thoughts, their work.

As I returned to the parish that morning of the fire, however, I was confident the family would rebuild both their lives and home. They belonged to strong, caring communities that would surround them with the support and help they would need in the task. Their strength and determination would receive a critical boost from those communities: school, work, and especially, their church community.

When I returned to the parish offices, the staff had already fielded dozens of phone calls from people offering help, everything from places for the family to stay to meal preparation. Each day, the mail brought generous check after generous check, and the recovery fund for the family grew larger. The doorbell constantly rang, announcing yet another donation of clothing, food, or household items to replace what had been lost.

As the efforts to assist the family continued, the liturgical decorations in our church building became even more meaningful to all of us. Every year, as November begins with the feast days of All Saints and All Souls, the folks in the parish put up the "paper people"—an unbroken string of nine hundred paper cutouts of people, linked hand in hand. Each "paper person" has the name of one of the nine hundred families that make up the parish written on it. This chain circles the walls of our church and is joined to a tapestry of Jesus that hangs on the back wall of our sanctuary, a powerful reminder that we are a family, spiritual brothers and sisters, and that our strength comes from one another. We have linked our lives to Jesus Christ as our teacher and our way. Young and old, black and white, sinner and saint, straight and gay, rich and poor, educated and uneducated, male and female, Republican and Democrat—all united together as one community with Jesus as leader and head.

When one person here suffers in any way, the whole community rallies to share its support and resources. St. Paul, describing what the church community is, writes, "Now you are Christ's body, and individually parts of it. If [one] part suffers, all the parts suffer with it; if one part is honored, all the parts share its joy" (1 Corinthians 12:26-27).

So often when bad things happen to good folks like Bill, Sandra, and their children, we wrestle with the apparent absence of God in the painful struggles of his people. Why didn't God raise his hand and prevent that fire? Why didn't God reverse its devastation? Why would God allow his people to know such fear? Doesn't God owe his people his personal attention? Why doesn't he inoculate us against pain and tragedy? We have all heard these hard questions, and we have all asked them.

We ask these questions more to vent our anger than out of a search for an answer. We ask them as a way to open a discussion about God's role in human suffering, as a way to engage others in conversation about God that will reassure us that he indeed is with us.

God is not absent. God is present. With the rare exceptions of Jesus' miracles, ranging from his raising of Lazarus from the dead to the feeding of the five thousand, God chooses to be present primarily through the community of his church.

On occasion, we come across dramatic stories of God's intervention in human struggle and storm, such as the incredible story of the parting of the Red Sea that allowed the Israelites to escape the pursuing Egyptians. But most often God chooses to be present in and to intervene through his church. The church community has power, capital, resources, and a strength that no one person could possibly possess, and God uses these things.

The church community offers the most of all the varied human communities we belong to. The reason is obvious. Like other communities, it offers assistance in meeting the material needs of people coping with loss and devastation. But more importantly, it ministers to their spiritual needs. In suffering, the church finds meaning. In death, the church proclaims life. In despair, the church gives hope. In the search for meaning to human existence, the church offers answers—answers it firmly believes are from God.

St. Paul defined the church as "the body of Christ." Christ's physical body is no longer present in the world. But Christ founded the church community and intended it to be his spiritual body, remaining in the world for every age and generation to follow. It is this church community, the body of Christ, that is God's primary presence in the world today.

In the wake of human tragedies and suffering, some would say, "God, why don't you do something about this terrible suffering?"

And God's reply? "I did. I made you!"

CHAPTER TWENTY-TWO

Not a Micromanager!

One would think that the great saints of the Christian faith would have the healthiest relationship with God. But that was often not the case. Like anyone else, the saints experienced the ups and downs of any loving relationship, and at times, when things weren't going smoothly, they felt anger and frustration with God.

A story about St. Teresa of Avila, a sixteenth-century Carmelite nun, provides a humorous example. St. Teresa was respected, not only in her native Spain but throughout the Christian world, as a deeply spiritual woman of prayer, contemplation, and love of neighbor. By all accounts, she was a woman very, very close to God.

One day St. Teresa gathered up two large baskets of food from her convent garden and kitchen. She set off to take this gift to a nearby village whose residents had lost everything in a flood. It was a typical act of caring that flowed out of her deep love for God.

As she made her way along a very muddy path that followed the swollen river into the village, she suddenly lost her footing and tumbled down the bank into the river. Both baskets of food were lost in the swift current, and St. Teresa had all she could do to swim to the shore, drag herself up the muddy bank, and regain the safety of the path.

Her food gone and her clothing drenched, Teresa was very, very angry with God. Covered with mud and shivering from the icy cold of the river, she knelt down on the path to pray: "My God, my God. No wonder you have so few friends, when you treat the ones you do have so badly!"[7]

St. Teresa's angry railing against God was more of a knee-jerk reaction to unexpected pain than it was a serious attempt to lay the blame at God's feet. Teresa knew it wasn't God who had built the villagers' homes too near the river. It wasn't God who had pushed her down the riverbank into the water. But in her frustration, she needed to lash out at someone. Who better to lash out at than the One she knew most loved her? God doesn't stop loving us because we have a temper tantrum and say hurtful things. No one is safer to be angry with.

Many people have done what St. Teresa did—lashed out at God in the midst of pain.

I had a good relationship with fifteen-year-old Debbie, a sophomore in our school. When we ran across each other during the school day, we smiled, exchanged a few words, and often told each other the latest joke we'd heard. Occasionally, when she was having a rough day, she would stop by my office for a quick cry and a sympathetic ear.

Debbie was the apple of her father's eye—his princess. Debbie worshipped him. He was her strength, her motivation, her inspiration. When she doubted herself, he encouraged her.

When she received word that her father had suffered a heart attack and died, Debbie was ill-equipped to deal with the shocking and unexpected news. She'd had no warning, no time to prepare. The news of his death slammed into her with terrifying force.

I offered Debbie some words of faith and my shoulder to

cry on, but when she returned to school a few days after the funeral, her head down and her shoulders slumped, she shrank away from me and the other friends who reached out to her. There was little life in her eyes.

As she drew deeper and deeper inside herself, I was stymied in my attempts to reach her. When I spotted her in the halls, she would turn and go the other way. When I sent notes to her homeroom, asking her to drop by the office for a talk, there was no reply and no Debbie. On the few occasions when she couldn't avoid me, she remained tightlipped except to mumble that she was all right and didn't want to talk.

Then one afternoon I found a letter from Debbie on my desk chair. It read in part:

Dear Father,

I want to apologize. I know that you feel you did something to make me upset at you, but you didn't. I'm not mad at you. I'm mad at God. I am so confused and have so many questions. Why did my father have to die? Why not somebody else? Why not me? He never did anything wrong. If I were to die, would I see him again? But most of all, if there is this wonderful person called God, then why did he let this happen? I used to think that God was the most important person in my life, even more important than my father. I don't anymore. I'm not even sure that there is a God....

I've saved Debbie's letter for a number of years now. I've saved it because, in just a couple of brief paragraphs, she expresses the questions, the doubts, and the universal anger we all feel when things go terribly wrong in our lives, when we are faced with soul-shaking traumas that leave us limp and helpless. It may be the death of one we love; it may be a natural disaster that wipes out a whole neighborhood. It may be a lingering and painful illness; it may be the loss of a job or a severe financial setback. It may be the onset of a powerful depression; it may be the breakup of our marriage. These traumas bring us to a turning point in our walk with God where we either let go of his hand and reject him, or we grasp his hand even more tightly and draw closer to him.

God is neither cruel nor absent. God doesn't will, cause, or bring about the things that go terribly wrong in our lives. God is not the problem; he's the solution. He has a master plan for this world, set into motion by his Son, Jesus Christ. Jesus gave a name to that plan: the kingdom of God.

In the early chapters of the book of Genesis, we read the divinely inspired story about Adam and Eve rejecting the perfect creation that God placed them in. Their rejection resulted in the imperfect world that we know all too well today. This was our choice. Our ancestors of faith—indeed, we ourselves—turned our backs on the perfect creation of Eden. We cast God and his dominion out of our lives and recreated his world into one of our own making, and it quickly spun out of control. We are the source of evil and suffering, not God.

God is not the villain in this sad story of human misery and misfortune. Quite the contrary, God is the hope for a way out of the morass. The kingdom of God will one day bring about a new Eden, a world without suffering and evil. Every day, the kingdom of God is closer to completion. Far from being cruel or absent in our lives, God is very present. But he doesn't micro-manage the master plan; the management is up to each one of us. And every act of compassion, every work of love diminishes the world's suffering and places another building stone in the construction of the kingdom of God.

CHAPTER TWENTY-THREE

God Is Only One Floor Away

A man found a cocoon of an emperor moth and took it home so he could witness the moth emerging from it. One day he noticed a small opening in the cocoon. He sat down and watched for hours as the creature struggled to force its body through the little hole. Then he noted that it seemed to have stopped making any progress.

It appeared to the man that the moth had gotten as far as it could in breaking out of the cocoon; it seemed hopelessly stuck. Out of genuine kindness, he decided to intervene. He took a pair of scissors and cut away the rest of the cocoon. The moth did emerge, but it had a swollen body and small, shriveled and undeveloped wings.

The man continued to watch the moth, expecting that in time the wings would enlarge and expand to be able to support the body, which would simultaneously shrink to its proper size. Neither of these things happened. In fact, the moth spent the rest of its life crawling around with a swollen body and shriveled wings. It was never able to fly.

Despite his good intentions, the man had failed to understand that the restricting cocoon and the moth's struggle to squeeze through the tiny opening were part of God's plan to force fluid from the body into the wings. Only when it had gone through this struggle and freed itself from the cocoon would the emperor moth be ready for flight.[8]

There's a powerful lesson in that story. Christians believe

that suffering and struggle play a role in our lives as we seek to be what God intends us to be. Sometimes we wish that God would remove our struggles and take away all of our obstacles. But just as that man crippled the emperor moth by seeking to remove its obstacles, so would we be crippled if God did that for us. He doesn't take away our problems and difficulties, but he does promise to be with us in the midst of them.

When I was a very small boy, my world was secure, protected, and comfortable. I knew little about the world beyond my home and family. It was enough for me to be at the center of my family's life. Then my parents dropped the bombshell. "The time has come," they said, "for you to begin school." And they enrolled me in the first grade at St. Margaret's.

My mother and I spent the days prior to school getting me fitted for my school uniform and buying a lunch pail, crayons, paper, a book bag, a coin purse to hold my recess candy money, and all the cute little things that a first grader takes to school on opening day. It was fun! I didn't have a clue as to the trauma that lay ahead.

On the appointed day, my mother reassuringly accompanied me. As we approached the front doors, a frightening figure loomed before us—a very formidable-looking nun, dressed in black habit and white wimple. My little Irish heart raced as it dawned on me that this woman would have control over my life for the next nine months.

I couldn't help but think of the story of the wicked witch, and I was sure that I was about to meet her in person. I saw behind the nun the faces of dozens of other little children, all under this woman's spell. They were staring at me. In a flash I went from being the center of my family's life to being just another one of the charges in this nun's care. She didn't know me; she didn't know how lovable and cute I was. She didn't have a clue that I was the most important person in my home.

Things only got bleaker when I realized I was going to have to share my world with dozens of other little kids, each of whom thought they were equally cute, lovable, and important.

My mother whispered some final words of encouragement, kissed me good-bye, and walked out the front door. I remember standing there, watching her leave. Somehow, Jesus' words on the cross came to my mind. "My God, my God, why have you forsaken me?" (Matthew 27:46). I was scared and felt keenly my mother's absence. I was also very, very angry with her.

What I didn't know that morning was that my mother was only a step away from me. She and the other first grade moms spent the morning in the basement hall with coffee and pastries, ready to spring into action if anything went wrong and their child needed them.

God does the same with us. He sometimes distances himself from us for the same reason my mother distanced herself from me. God has vested us with all the tools necessary for us to build a productive life for ourselves. It is up to us to begin the work and task that God has given us. Just as I would never have become a responsible, independent adult if my parents did my schoolwork, fought my battles, and dressed me in rainwear at recess time, so you and I would never learn lessons or accountability if God intervened every time we were about to make a mistake. If God prevented things from going wrong in our lives, we would not be the glory of his creation. We would simply be wooden, lifeless puppets attached to strings manipulated by God, the Divine Puppeteer. God will not interfere with our human freedom. In power and mystery, he invites rather than manipulates us to be loving people.

God remains near us in the human journey, but he also must put distance between us if we are ever to grow and become what he has made us to be. But I'll tell you, at times, as he watches us bumble along, it must give him divine heartburn not to intervene.

CHAPTER TWENTY-FOUR

And God Will Be There

I frequently speak to youngsters about how to recognize the presence of God in their everyday lives. There's a little gimmick that I am fond of using to capture their attention. I hold up a sign with these words boldly printed on it: GOD IS NOWHERE. Then I ask them to read what they see. Some will read it, "God is no-where." Others see it differently and read it, "God is now-here."

No two of us see reality in exactly the same way. We bring different experiences to our interpretations of what we see. Take, for example, three people who look at a tree. One might see the tree as so many cords of wood that will heat his house for a certain number of days. Another person might look at that same tree and see so many board feet of lumber that he can sell for a handsome profit. Yet a third person might look at that tree and see God's hand at work in the way it provides shade and rest for those who sit under its branches and in its beauty. It's the same tree, but people will view it in vastly different ways according to their diverse needs, agendas, and values.

The same dynamic is at work when it comes to recognizing the presence of God in our everyday lives. Some can only recognize God's presence in a church setting; others can only see God's presence in the majesty of nature. Still others can't recognize God's presence anywhere and conclude that there is no God.

"Hey, Father!"

As a priest, I've been conditioned through both experience and training to see God's presence everywhere, every day. I'm not alone. Many have this same vision. Those with a jaundiced skepticism about God find it upsetting to listen to professional athletes or celebrities thank God and acknowledge his help in their achievement. They may wonder, *What does God have to do with a running back winning the MVP award at the Super Bowl?* Or, *What does God have to do with an actor winning an Oscar?* If you ask the athlete and actor, they will make eloquent cases for the hand and presence of God in their success. Skeptics will simply not understand because their experience, agenda, and values have conditioned them to see differently.

Some seven or eight years ago, our girl's basketball team won their first state championship. It was a big night for the school and the thousands of fans who had poured out on the court, much to the displeasure of the authorities, and mobbed the team and the coaches. It was all televised, and a reporter collared our coach for a statement. The crowd immediately quieted to hear his words. He began by saying, "First, I want to thank God!" At this our crowd went absolutely wild. They chanted God's name, applauded his presence. I thought to myself that this must be one of the very few times when God received more attention than the athletes. As a Christian school, we daily point to the presence of God among us, and we're conditioned to look for him.

One afternoon I arrived at my parish office and found a message on my desk asking for a priest to visit a dying man in the neighborhood. I didn't recognize the man's name, but it's not at all unusual for people who don't belong to any church to ask for a priest when death draws near. The poor man was very much alone; he was estranged from his family and had only recently arrived in town and had no community from which to draw support. In his early fifties, he had been diagnosed with terminal lung cancer and told he had a few short months to live. Even with government assistance, he couldn't keep up with his mounting bills and often went without the medication he needed.

When I went to see him, he told me he was a Catholic, but only in name. He had drifted away from the church as a young man, and more importantly, had drifted away from God. He had a lot of setbacks and misfortunes in his life, and they had left him bitter and more and more convinced that God was simply absent, aloof, and uncaring. But now he was dying. He told me that he had been revisiting and reexamining the meaningful moments of his past, one of which was his experience of being part of a church community as a youth. It was one of the very few times in his life where he had felt welcomed and valued for himself, a time when he felt very close to God and was very aware of God at work in his life.

He wanted only one thing from me: Christian burial. Normally, the state provides only a cremation service for those who die penniless. He desperately wanted to be buried in a plot in a Christian cemetery, preceded by a funeral service in church. He didn't want to die alone and forgotten; he wanted to die joined to the Christian community that had brought hope and meaning to his long-ago youth.

I didn't have the thousands of dollars necessary to grant his wish, but as I drove home, I realized where I could get it. The following Sunday, I shared some of his story with my parishioners at all the morning Masses. By Monday I was able to assure him of a Christian burial. The Catholic cemetery had donated his plot, the St. Vincent de Paul Society in the parish had pledged to pay all funeral expenses, and the people in the pews gave enormous gifts of money that made it possible for the man to buy the medicine he needed, to pay his rent, and to have a few luxury comforts to ease his final days. Chore ministers—people from the parish who volunteer their time and elbow grease—regularly visited the man to clean his apartment, cook his meals, and take him to his doctor's appointments. Often, when I would stop by to bring him Holy Communion and visit, he would comment, "I don't know why I waited so many years to ask for God's help."

When he died, our church celebrated the funeral Mass of the Resurrection. The pews were filled with the folks who had brought God's caring, compassionate presence to this man's final days. "God is love, and whoever remains in love remains in God and God in him" (1 John 4:16).

CHAPTER TWENTY-FIVE

Glimpses of God in Intensive Care

I recently received a phone call from a young woman asking if I would be the priest at her upcoming wedding. She began the conversation saying, "Father, this is Loriann. I don't know if you remember me, but ..."

How could I forget Loriann? I met her at the beginning of a new semester when she strolled into my religion class two minutes after the bell. I wanted to clearly set the boundaries and my expectations for the class, so I called her over to my desk and reminded her that being late for class was not acceptable.

But Loriann didn't have patience with teachers who wasted her time by pointing out her shortcomings. She had a sharp tongue for a fifteen-year-old, and she wasn't about to hold it in check for the likes of me. She let me know exactly what she thought of my little rule about punctuality. Few things irritate me more than a snippy attitude, so as Loriann started to lay out her defense, I rolled my eyes heavenward as if seeking divine relief from this latest exasperation.

That did it. Loriann put her hands on my desk, got right in my face, and rolled her eyes right back at me, as if to say, "You're pretty hard to take yourself."

Surprisingly, our confrontation established an immediate mutual respect and we developed a good friendship. Every time we passed in the halls, saw each other in class, met each other at a ball game, or encountered each other at church or in the shopping mall, we immediately rolled our eyes to the heavens. Then we would break into a big smile and start talking. Even today, many years later, we always roll our eyes at each other.

One evening when she was a senior, Loriann was returning home with a friend from a school dance. Just a mile away from home, she lost control of her car and went through the front of a store. Seriously injured, she was rushed by ambulance to Seattle's Harborview Hospital. A few hours later, her parents called and asked if I would come to the intensive care ward and administer our church's sacrament of the anointing of the sick for their daughter.

When I arrived at the hospital, I went straight to the desk of the intensive care wing and asked if I could see Loriann. I was directed to one of six beds on the ward. I didn't even recognize her. Her face was badly swollen and misshapen. Bandages were wrapped around her head and casts encased her arms. She was hooked up to multiple machines by plastic tubing. Nearby, monitors beeped quietly.

I bent over her and whispered her name. Her eyes fluttered for a moment and then remained open, though it took her a moment to focus. She couldn't talk because of the ventilator, but she clearly knew who was at her bedside. She rolled her eyes at me and I saw the beginning of a smile, despite the tape that held the breathing tube in place. I immediately rolled my eyes back at her and began the prayers of our church.

A few days later, the tubes were removed and Loriann was moved to a regular room. Her injuries had been severe, but nothing that wouldn't heal over time. I went back to visit her, and she talked about her ordeal. She felt terrified from the moment she woke up in her car. The ambulance ride, the rush into the emergency room on a stretcher, the crush of doctors and nurses cutting off her clothing, the probing and prodding, being wheeled into the operating room, and finally waking up surrounded by strange people and sounds—it all frightened her. She wasn't sure she was going to make it, and because she couldn't speak, she wasn't able to ask the questions that might bring her reassurance.

In the midst of her racing fears, she said, she heard someone whisper her name. She opened her eyes and saw a face, a goofy-looking priest who had always rolled his eyes at her. At that moment, she knew that she was not alone, and she knew she was going to be OK. She rolled her eyes to heaven—only this time it wasn't a feigned gesture of exasperation. It was a genuine gesture of thanksgiving for God's presence in the midst of her terrifying struggle.

I've administered the sacrament to many hospitalized students. Every time, my heart races; I know their young lives are in jeopardy. I always pray that God will give me the right words to ease the family's fears as well as the patient's, but I rarely talk about my own fears. When I see one of my students so vulnerable, so fragile, so near death, so dependent on others, I get a lump in my throat and feel a weight in my heart that makes it difficult to speak. I need God's peace and calming and reassurance just as much as the patient needs mine.

How do I reach my own place of calm? The very first thing I do with the patient, and later with the family, is to pray Psalm 139. The words of that psalm beautifully proclaim an ever-present God. Verse five reads, "Behind and before you encircle me and rest your hand upon me."

Once I'm centered on the ever-present God, I am calm enough to reassure the patient and the family that with God's help, we will all get through this crisis. Only when I've reached my own place of calm am I able to point out where God can be found in the situation.

In Loriann's case, God's presence was visible in her mother, sleeping on a cot next to her hospital bed. God's presence was unmistakable in the group of her classmates tightly wedged into the tiny waiting room outside the intensive care ward. It was there in the face of the very serious-looking doctor reading over her medical chart.

And according to Loriann, God's presence was with her, too, in the form of a goofy-looking priest, rolling his eyes toward heaven.

SECTION SIX

"Hey, Father!
What's Most Important in Life?"

CHAPTER TWENTY-SIX

Earthquakes Have Messages

I have a favorite story I'm fond of telling at weddings: a young boy and his father are sitting on the couch on a rainy day, leafing through the family photo album. The boy comes across a picture of his mother on her wedding day. She's young and beautiful, dressed in a dazzling white gown, her face radiant and joyful. The boy stares at the picture for a long time and then turns to his father and asks, "Daddy, is this the day that mom came to work for us?"

We so easily take our treasures for granted!

As a young priest I was hospitalized for the first time in my life, confined to a hospital bed for three straight months. My window overlooked a small lake that was popular with joggers and strollers of all ages. How jealous I was of their ability to simply walk around the lake on a sunny afternoon! Up to that point in my life, I had never given a moment's thought to my legs. They had always worked. But when they stopped working, believe me, I thought about them. Getting my legs to function again was the most important thing in my life.

In 1989, a very serious earthquake rocked San Francisco, killing a number of people. Bridges collapsed, buildings tumbled down and highways broke apart. It was called the "World Series Quake" because, among its minor disruptions, it led to the cancellation of a World Series baseball game at San Francisco's Candlestick Park. The earthquake left many people grieving and homeless. The city had a temporary food shortage and daily life was disrupted for weeks.

"Hey, Father!"

On the Sunday evening after the earthquake, one of the stories on national TV news featured a Catholic church that had been destroyed in the quake. The parishioners had come together to celebrate the Sunday morning Mass in the parking lot of the church. They sat on folding lawn chairs and hunks of concrete that had once been the walls of their house of worship. Piles of rubble stood in the background.

The television camera captured the pain and shock in their faces as they listened to their pastor: "My friends, all of us have suffered a great deal in the past few days. Some of you have lost your homes; some of you have lost all your earthly possessions. We have even lost our church building. But none of us has lost anything of lasting or eternal value. We still have our lives. We still have the love that binds us together as the family of God. We still have our faith in God and our hope that God will be our strength and refuge in the days to come. We have lost nothing that really matters in our lives."

That gentle, elderly priest had magnificently articulated what is really important in the human journey. Homes can be rebuilt, possessions can be replaced, streets can be swept clean of rubble and debris, bridges and roadways can be repaired, cities can be put back together. There may have been a time when we thought these material things really mattered. Perhaps you have yelled at the kids for tracking mud into your precious house or got upset with your husband when he accidentally dropped that family heirloom vase. But faith, hope, and love are what truly matter. No force on earth can destroy these treasures or take them away from us.

"So faith, hope, love remain, these three; but the greatest of these is love," wrote St. Paul (1 Corinthians 13:13). While I have neither St. Paul's wisdom or special position with God, I respectfully disagree with part of what he wrote. To select love as the greatest of the three is akin to having three children and selecting one of them as the best. All three—faith, hope, and love—are equally great and equally essential in human life.

Faith, hope, and love anchor our life in bedrock, allowing us to ride out any storm that comes around, any disaster, natural or human. These treasures can't be purchased with any credit card, no matter the limit. They can't be found on the shelf of any department store or accessed online. They come only from God, and they occupy a position in the center and deepest part of our soul. If we choose to unwrap these three spiritual gifts and connect our lives to their power, they will shape us into what God designed us to be: creatures fashioned in his own image and likeness.

Many of us take these gifts for granted. Their central importance gets lost in the barrage of messages and images that surround us as we go about our daily lives. The image makers and advertisers would have us believe that what really matters is the car we drive, the college we attend, the suburb we live in, the clothes we wear, the amount of hair on our heads, the number of pounds on our bodies, the size of our portfolio, the credit limit on our plastic cards.

Deep within us we reject these superficial and plastic substitutes. We know that the pursuit of and obsession with inconsequential "things" take us away from our center. Unfortunately, only when what really matters is jeopardized in some way are we able to see faith, hope, and love as our life anchors.

Maybe we need more earthquakes in our lives.

CHAPTER TWENTY-SEVEN

The Search for Meaning

It's in every priest's contract with God that we stand outside the church after Sunday morning Masses to connect in a small way with each of our departing parishioners. God knew what he was doing; a lot of work gets thrown our way during those thirty minutes.

Most of these Sunday morning exchanges are mundane: updates on family news, requests to bless new cars, suggestions for improvements on my sermon, invitations to dinner, complaints about the music or the heat or the broken pew. That sort of thing. Occasionally, though, a conversation stays with me long after everyone has gone home.

One Sunday I spotted a young woman coming out of the church with two small children in tow. I had never seen her before, so I walked over to introduce myself and find out who she was. As we talked, she let drop that this was the first time she had been to church since her first year in college. I was curious: what had prompted her to come to Mass this particular morning?

She pointed to the children and said, "Father, I have these two small children now. I desperately want them to understand that there is more meaning to their lives than what they find in the shopping malls."

Her words beautifully captured the universal search of every generation to find meaning in their lives and the disenchantment that inevitably comes when we latch on to easy and immediate answers. Marketers tell us we can find meaning for our lives in the "stuff" that crowds the shelves in their stores. We get bombarded with the message that one simply can't have a truly meaningful life without a television, a computer, the latest fashions, or the newest electronic wonder.

The young mother I was speaking with had gone this route and found it sorely wanting. She didn't want her children to come to the place she'd come to, disillusioned with the glittering but hollow answers of the shopping malls. She had come to church that morning to revisit and search out the answers of the faith community to the hunger she felt—a hunger to understand life's meaning and experience a meaningful life.

As we talked, I remembered the story of the great St. Augustine, the classic model for every man and woman in search of a meaningful life.

St. Augustine was one of the greatest intellectuals and teachers of early Christianity. He didn't reach this status, however, without one heck of a twisting journey. Born in A.D. 354 in Tagaste, North Africa, Augustine was reared as a Christian by his mother, St. Monica, but eventually he rejected Christianity and its answers to life's meaning. Whether his desertion of the faith was based on the rebellion of youth or honest intellectual inquiry is unclear.

Hungry to find his own answers, Augustine carved out a career for himself pursuing that passion. He became a teacher of rhetoric and philosophy in Milan, a convenient platform for his search. The meaningful life continued to elude him, and like many before and after him, he found temporary solace in the immediate pleasures of the fourth century equivalent of shopping malls. Wine, women, song, and the party life were not what he was looking for, but they were an attractive comfort while he searched.

When he reached his midthirties, depressed about the shallow and purposeless life he seemed to be leading and discouraged about finding any answers beyond what he had already found, Augustine experienced a profound and life-changing conversion.

One account of his conversion I particularly like, although it is not grounded in historical fact. In the midst of his depression, according to the story, Augustine was mulling over the people in his life whom he most admired, the ones who seemed most contented with their lives. Ranked first on his list was his mother, St. Monica. At the center of her life was God, the God revealed by Jesus. Her relationship with God, it seemed, was the source of her great compassion and kindness, her serenity and peaceful spirit, her selflessness and inner joy. Time spent with God in prayer and meditation was as much a part of her daily life as eating.

But Augustine was fearful of letting go of the pleasures and "things" that crowded his life in order to make room for the demands of a relationship with God. He went to a nearby monastery and sought out the abbot, who was his mother's spiritual director, asking the old priest how he could bring God into his life.

The saintly man answered Augustine's question by taking him down to the river and wading in, beckoning Augustine to follow. When they were both in water up to their shoulders, the abbot grabbed Augustine's head and held it under with his strong arms. The younger man struggled, but the priest was too strong. Finally he released Augustine, who bobbed to the surface, gasping for air and spitting out water.

When they returned to the shore, the old abbot asked, "What did you want more than anything while you were under the water?" Augustine replied, "Air!" The priest smiled and said, "My son, when you want God as badly as you wanted air, that is when you will find room for him in your life."

It was the turning point in Augustine's life, the story goes. He let go of the clutter clogging his spirit and made room for God and an ongoing relationship with him.

A more accurate account of Augustine's conversion is found in his own autobiography, *Confessions.* While in his mid-thirties, he came under the influence of St. Ambrose, who was the bishop of Milan. Ambrose was a brilliant man, powerfully persuasive in articulating the Christian message. More importantly, he was an intensely spiritual man who, like Augustine's mother, found meaning for his life first and foremost in his relationship with God. Ambrose continually encouraged Augustine to revisit the Christian faith of his youth and find the answers he was searching for in its truth.

The turning point came one day while Augustine was walking in his garden. He spotted his mother's Bible lying on a nearby table. His eyes seemed to be drawn to it, and he heard a small voice within him say, "Pick it up and read."

He obeyed the voice. The Bible fell open to this passage from St. Paul:

Now the works of the flesh are obvious: immorality, impurity, licentiousness, idolatry, sorcery, hatreds, rivalry, jealousy, outbursts of fury, acts of selfishness, dissensions, factions, occasions of envy, drinking bouts, orgies, and the like. I warn you, as I have warned you before, that those who do such things will not inherit the kingdom of God. In contrast, the fruit of the Spirit is love, joy, peace, patience, kindness, generosity, faithfulness, gentleness, and self-control.

GALATIANS 5:19-23a

These words from the New Testament were the sign he was looking for. They expressed perfectly where Augustine had been, and they also expressed where he wanted to be—the place that his mother, St. Monica, and his mentor, St. Ambrose, already resided. Realizing he had found what he'd been looking for, he uttered the prayer that he is most famous for: "Oh God, my heart is restless, until it rests in Thee."

Truer words were never spoken.

CHAPTER TWENTY-EIGHT

It's All About the Heart

Three college students were having a late lunch off campus before their afternoon lab class. One of them checked his watch and noticed that time had gotten away from them; they had less than three minutes before the mandatory class was to begin. The three jumped up from their table and began a mad dash through the streets to the science building. As they rounded a corner, they accidentally brushed a table on the sidewalk. A basket of apples tumbled to the pavement and the apples went bouncing down the street. The students saw that a blind girl had been sitting at the table selling the fruit, but they didn't stop. They were more afraid of the wrath of their professor than they were of the young girl.

They made it to the classroom just as the bell rang, but one of the students didn't go in. Ashamed of his callous and indifferent behavior toward the blind girl, he retraced his steps and found her on her hands and knees with tears in her eyes, trying to retrieve the spilled fruit by feel. He apologized for his and his friends' conduct, grabbed the basket, and filled it with the scattered apples. Noting that some of the fruit was bruised and damaged, he gave the girl enough money to pay for the whole basket. As he turned to leave, the blind girl grabbed his sleeve and said, "Hey, mister! Are you Jesus?"[9]

When people encountered Jesus, they experienced a man who brought compassion to their lives. The sick, the possessed, the poor, the outcast, the diseased, the mentally ill—all came face-to-face with tender compassion in the presence of

Jesus. "At the sight of the crowds, his heart was moved with pity for them because they were troubled and abandoned, like sheep without a shepherd" (Matthew 9:36).

One of the most popular images in Catholic religious art is that of the "sacred heart of Jesus," a bleeding heart portrayed on the outside of Jesus' chest. Many of our churches have statues of Jesus depicting his sacred heart. Paintings often show his heart alone. Many of our parishes are named the Church of the Sacred Heart; four parishes in the Archdiocese of Seattle alone share this name.

When I was a small child, the image of Jesus with a bleeding heart on his chest frightened me. When I was a teenager, it no longer scared me, but I found it too saccharine and overly pious for my taste. Only later, as an adult, did I begin to appreciate how well and how appropriately the image captures the very essence of Jesus' life and teachings. The heart is the universally recognized symbol of love. Love was the centerpiece of Jesus' message—of both his words and his example. If there is any one image that points to what Jesus' life was all about, it has to be the heart.

Almost all of us have had the wondrous experience of lying on our back on a summer evening and staring up at the night sky, filled with twinkling stars and planets. Something about a summer night sky stirs deep questions: Why are we here? What is the meaning of my existence? Is my life purposeful? If so, what is its purpose?

God has an answer to those great questions. Two critically important verses of Scripture lay the foundation for the answer to every question about our purpose in life: "Then God said: 'Let us make man in our image, after our likeness....'

God created man in his image; in the divine image he created him; male and female he created them" (Genesis 1:26-27). "God is love, and whoever remains in love, remains in God and God in him" (1 John 4:16).

We are made in the image and likeness of God. God is love. The inescapable conclusion is that we are to be lovers. Insofar as we love, our lives reflect their divine design. When we fail to love, our lives reject their God-given meaning.

In Jesus we have the living answer to our questions about life's meaning. Jesus' life was a model for all to study, examine, and emulate. The crux of his message was, "This is who God wants you to be." If we look carefully at Jesus, we'll see a man with his heart on his chest.

Years ago I visited Florence. Our tour guide took us to see Michelangelo's magnificent statue of David, sculpted by the great Italian artist in 1502. David's body is youthful and powerful, every muscle and sinew brimming with raw might and vitality. As we studied the impressive work, the guide remarked that often when people look at the statue, they instinctively stand taller, throw their shoulders back, and tighten their stomach. Sure enough, that's what I was doing. When we look at an image or example of what we could be if we were in top, prime physical condition, our reflexes take over and our body is driven to imitate what it sees.

When we enter into a relationship with Christ, we find the answer to all our questions about life's purpose: we are to imitate him. As we examine and study Jesus' life, we quickly discover that his heart is the sum and substance of who he is. As we gaze at the sacred heart of Jesus, our hearts soften. And in the act of loving, we find genuine meaning for our lives.

CHAPTER TWENTY-NINE

The Left Foot of Jesus

At the beginning of each new school year, one of my jobs is to assemble the latest crop of freshmen in our chapel for an orientation on the religious mission of our school. One of the first things I do is call their attention to a huge, carved wooden statue that stands on a pedestal in a back corner—a statue of a proud and somewhat tired-looking St. Joseph with his arm around the shoulder of the boy Jesus.

"Do you notice anything unusual about this statue?" I ask. It doesn't take long before one of them notices the left foot of Jesus, obviously once broken and somewhat haphazardly re-attached with glue.

Stories and images are a wonderful door into the mystery of spirituality, especially for youngsters. The broken foot always stirs my students' curiosity, making their hearts ripe for the story I have to tell.

I don't know how Jesus broke his foot originally; my guess is that it happened when the statue was transported here from Italy. For as long as I had been at the school, the break line where the foot had been reattached was visible. We were all accustomed to it.

Jesus with a broken foot I can live with, but Jesus with a missing foot was a different matter. One morning some twenty-five years ago, as I walked into the chapel to prepare for the morning Mass, something about the statue caught my eye. I paused in front of it, certain something was amiss. My eyes were drawn to the young Jesus, and sure enough, all was not well—the Son of God was balancing precariously on his right foot! All that remained where his broken left foot had been were his ankle and some crusty glue residue.

I was shocked and angry. Obviously someone in our community was responsible for this kidnapping of Jesus' foot, and I was determined to get to the bottom of the crime. No one should get away with a prank like that.

But I had no clues, no leads. The school year ended, and then another and yet another. I finally abandoned all hope of solving the puzzle and resigned myself to a statue of Jesus without a left foot. After all, the Vatican museums house lots of statuary missing all kinds of body parts, and people come from all over the world to see them. Maybe our statue of Jesus would take on new status in the art world.

Three years and four months after Jesus' foot disappeared, on the morning of graduation, one of our seniors dropped by my office. Beth and I were good friends. While many students listened politely to my jokes, I got the feeling most of them laughed at the proper time and then went away feeling as if they had done their good deed for the day. Beth, on the other hand, actually enjoyed my humor.

On this graduation morning, Beth and I had a long, pleasant conversation tracing back over the memories of the last four years. But as she got up to leave, her voice began to quiver and tears began to form. When I asked her what was wrong, she said, "Father, there's something I have to tell you before I graduate tonight, and I'm afraid you're going to be awfully angry." With that, she reached into a bag and pulled out the long-missing foot of Jesus.

I was as shocked at that moment as I was the morning I had discovered Jesus' foot was gone. Beth would have been the very last one on my suspect list. All I could say was, "Beth, why?"

She had a lot of tears that morning, but not much of an answer. During lunch she and a good friend had been in the chapel, a favorite place not only for students to pray but sometimes to talk quietly with a trusted friend. She hadn't planned on taking Jesus' foot, but as they got up to leave she spotted it just barely clinging to his ankle. On a whim she liberated it and stuffed it into her schoolbag. It was an impulse, an adolescent prank.

Who really knows what goes on in the mind of fourteen-year-olds? Teenagers don't process things with the same clarity that adults do. It takes them a bit longer to understand the consequences of their choices. To Beth's credit, when what she had done sank in a few hours later, she had every intention of returning it to its place in the chapel. But she kept putting it off with the customary mantra of many teenagers: "I'll do it tomorrow." Beth's "tomorrow" had taken over three years to arrive.

What prompted Beth to return the foot before she graduated? I like to think it was because she possessed something even more important than Jesus' foot—she had Jesus' heart. Bringing the foot back and admitting what she had done was evidence to me of Jesus' heart at work in her.

When I tell the freshmen this story, I use it as a springboard to explain that each of us is called by God to be the presence of Jesus in our world. We are to be his feet, his hands, his shoulders, his arms, his heart. Jesus isn't in the wood of a statue. He is in his disciples who minister in his name.

In the sanctuary of our chapel, hanging from the wall, is a colorful, quilted banner showing a number of hands attached to a vine. Each hand has a quality of Jesus written on it:

compassion, service, mercy, forgiveness, justice, love, and so forth. Underneath is a biblical reference, John 15:5: "I am the vine and you are the branches. Whoever remains in me and I in him will bear much fruit."

The banner was made by one of our teachers, who was inspired by a story that was a centerpiece of a school liturgy celebrating the theme of service. In the waning days of World War II, a group of American soldiers entered a small German village that had been virtually flattened by bombs. They decided to bivouac for the night in the badly damaged but still standing village church. Off to the side of the sanctuary was a statue of Jesus, intact except for the arms, which had been blown off. Around the neck of the statue, someone had placed a sign written crudely in German: "You must now be my hands."[10]

Beth graduated fifteen years before that banner went up in our sanctuary. But I have to believe that her time with the "borrowed" left foot of Jesus left her with a similar message. She went on to become a nurse, marry, and start a family. Occasionally I would receive a Christmas card from her, and rather than sign her name she would draw a little foot. In one of those cards, she shared with me her strong feeling that her nursing hands were the "hands of Jesus." When I reminded her recently of that comment, she said, "Father, I believe that with all my heart. In fact, early on in my nursing career I asked the chaplain at the hospital to bless and consecrate my hands. I truly mean them to be Jesus' hands."

Somehow I don't think Jesus minded his left foot being on loan to Beth. That loan has been repaid a hundredfold through the hands of a nurse who heals the broken in his name.

CHAPTER THIRTY

Leave Something Beautiful Behind

Discovery Park is a large and beautiful park near my home in Seattle. It borders on Puget Sound, and the land has been left undeveloped. The name is a bit of a misnomer, as it's one of the least discovered parks in the city.

Almost every day I walk my dogs, Abraham and Isaac, on the park trails—or more precisely, Abraham and Isaac pull and drag me down the trails. On our daily adventures, I frequently come across an elderly and frail-looking gentleman who lives in the neighborhood. He must be close to ninety, but nearly every day, rain or shine, he is in the park as a volunteer, clearing brush and planting little trees and shrubs. When he finishes one section, he moves on and begins improving another. Because the park is so large, it would take ten of his lifetimes of service to make a noticeable difference.

Every time my walk takes me past this old man who labors anonymously and generously for others, we exchange pleasantries. I've always wanted to ask him why he does this work day after day, but I never have. Somehow it seems too private and personal. At ninety, he certainly isn't going to live long enough to see the results of all his labor; he'll be long dead by the time his carefully planted and lovingly tended trees and shrubs grow tall and blossom. But if I had the courage to ask him, I imagine this generous man would reply, "I want to leave something beautiful behind."

Most of us desire to leave the world better off for our having lived in it, to leave something that says, "I was here and I made a difference." It seems right, for the world has been generous and giving to us. We are the recipients and benefactors of its resources and life-sustaining treasures. We naturally want to give back as a gesture of our gratitude. We want to know that others will be enriched in some small way by the gifts we give, whether the planting of a tree or a substantial check to charity.

A few years ago, we invited a retired minister from Seattle's University Congregational Church to be the commencement speaker at our high school's graduation. Dr. Dale Turner is a powerful speaker and a well-respected citizen in our community. His challenge to our graduates that year still circles around in my head today: "Do something each day, at a cost to yourself, for someone else." If each of our seniors, some 250 young people, did what he asked, what an impact they would have in this world during their lifetimes! Do the math—it's an incredible number of acts of kindness.

Some months later, as we sat around the fireplace the first night of a high school retreat, I mentioned Dr. Turner's words and invited the students to share their most memorable experience of someone they knew doing something for another at a cost to self. Jason was the first to volunteer. He settled into our special chair in the center of the group and recalled this story:

His father had picked Jason up after baseball practice to take him to a Mariner's baseball game at the old Kingdome in Seattle. It was raining heavily and they were running late. As they neared the stadium, they spotted a man lying very nearly in the gutter, his legs dangerously close to traffic. A bottle of wine was in one of his hands, and it appeared he had passed out from drinking.

Jason's father immediately pulled over to the curb, unbuckled his seat belt and started to get out of the car. Jason protested, "Dad, we're going to be late for the game." His father either didn't hear him or chose not to hear him. "Come on, Jason, give me a hand," he urged.

The man reeked of alcohol, vomit speckled his coat, the rain plastered his hair to his head, and his speech was semi-coherent, but he was able to tell them where he lived. Jason, although embarrassed and somewhat disgusted by the drunk, helped his father get him into their car, and they headed for the address, less than a mile away.

Supporting him on either side, father and son managed to escort the poor man to his rundown room in a seedy hotel. Once inside, the man flopped down on his bed and went to sleep. Jason's father fished a twenty-dollar bill out of his wallet and left it on the dresser. They were late for the game, but suddenly Jason didn't mind anymore.

He was ashamed of his initial reluctance to help the man, but his father didn't mention it. In fact, he and his father never really talked about the incident. But it had a profound effect on him, Jason told us. Not only was he tremendously proud of his father, but his father's example that night would serve as his personal moral compass for the rest of his life. It had shaken loose his preoccupation with himself and helped him to see in a new way the needs of people around him.

What Jason saw in his father that night was a Christ figure, for Jesus' life was a life of service, at a cost to himself, for others. Jesus said, "Give and gifts will be given to you; a good measure, packed together, shaken down, and overflowing, will be poured into your lap. For the measure with which you measure will in return be measured out to you" (Luke 7:38).

Giving is one of the things that truly matters in our lives. Not only does giving make this a much better world, but giving makes us much better people. It also brings powerful blessings into our lives. Jason's father invested an hour of his time and twenty dollars in a man he didn't know. He will never receive that hour nor the money back. But his example that rainy night touched his son in a way no words ever could have done. His son will carry on his legacy of kindness, and the world will continue to be renewed by the power of love.

The old man laboring in Discovery Park may never live long enough to see the fruit of his handiwork, but his example inspired this priest to sign up for the park work parties. Giving is one of the important things in life.

SECTION SEVEN

"Hey, Father!
How Can I Stop Hurting?"

CHAPTER THIRTY-ONE

When It Hurts Too Much to Live

I first met Ryland when he was a fourteen-year-old freshman. He wandered into my office after school one afternoon announcing that he was looking for the student bookstore. He was off by one floor and the length of our large building. That—coupled with the fact that my door has a sign over it that reads "Chaplain" in large letters—told me he wasn't really looking for the bookstore.

When I told him the bookstore was downstairs and down the hall, he nodded and started wandering around my office, occasionally asking questions about the extensive array of junk that hangs from my walls and ceiling and clutters my shelves and floor. My office doesn't have windows and its walls are a cold, institutional tile. Every square inch is covered with "stuff" I've collected over the last thirty years—pictures of students I've taught and wrestling teams I've coached; mementos of plays, proms, championships, retreats, Masses; old school athletic jerseys, plaques, awards, and T-shirts.

My collection seemed to fascinate Ryland, but I had a strong feeling that what he was really looking for was conversation with some adult figure at school who would listen seriously to what he was feeling and dreaming.

In the months and years that followed, Ryland and I became good friends. He would come to my office, throw himself into my overstuffed chair, stretch his long, bony legs across the floor, and make himself at home. We talked about everything during these visits: sports, philosophy, morality, movies, and life after high school. What Ryland didn't talk about was his pain. Looking back, I realize that perhaps I didn't ask the right questions. I wish I had.

Near Christmas of his sophomore year, Ryland bounced into my office and said, "Hey, Father! What size shoes do you wear?" Ever since I was a boy, people have kidded me about my big feet, and I thought Ryland was doing the same. "Eleven and a half and proud of it," I said. The day before school let out for Christmas vacation, Ryland came to see me with a big grin and a decorated package. "A little Christmas present, Father," he said. "You might want to open it now."

When I unwrapped it, I was as surprised as he was pleased. Inside was a shiny pair of new shoes that had to have set him back sixty dollars. Ryland had noticed that both my shoes had holes in the bottom of their soles and decided that a new pair would be the perfect gift for me. He loved puns, and his card read, "Father, maybe you should spend a little time looking after your own soles rather than everyone else's souls."

I told him how pleased I was with his gift, but a couple of things troubled me. One was that I'd given him the impression that I couldn't afford to buy new shoes, and he'd spent his own money to buy me some. The truth is that I simply hate to go shopping, so I wait until my clothes are in tatters and become the subject of conversation among those with too little to do. But Ryland must have felt my financial resources were the equivalent of someone living on the streets.

The other concern was that I absolutely hated the style of the shoes he'd picked out. I've always worn penny loafers, and Ryland had purchased wing tips—with miles of laces and embroidered designs in the leather. In my eyes they were ugly, heavy, and clumsy. Normally you couldn't pay me to wear shoes like that, but wear them I did—every day—until Ryland graduated. Why? Because he gave them to me.

As his high school years went by, Ryland grew in confidence, threw himself into all kinds of school activities, gained the respect of teachers and classmates, and spent time with the younger students. His senior year he was elected student body president.

On the outside, Ryland looked like he was doing great, but inside he was suffering. Yet in all our conversations, he never gave me a clue about the pain in his soul. His senior year ended with the usual flurry of events: the senior prom, senior skip day, baccalaureate, graduation, the all-night party that followed, and a host of parties over the next few days.

Then it all came apart.

About ten o'clock in the evening, several days after his graduation, alone and weighted down by his backpack, Ryland walked to the middle of the Aurora Bridge and jumped over the side.

The Aurora Bridge is the highest in Seattle and spans a canal that links Lake Washington to Puget Sound. It's a popular choice for people who want to commit suicide, and probably eight out of every ten who go over the side are killed. Ryland was not. Plucked out of the water by a passing boat, he was rushed to Harborview Hospital with critical injuries to his brain, spinal column, and some of his internal organs.

I had never met his mother, but she called the school and asked if "the priest that Ryland had given those shoes to" would come and pray for her son. When I walked into his room, I was shocked. He lay in a coma. The Ryland that I had teased and joked with just days before was unmoving, bruised, badly battered, and hooked up to a maze of machines that kept his body functioning. With his mother at my side I prayed, then took out my stole and the oil of the sick and administered the sacrament of the anointing of the sick. (Ryland wasn't Catholic, but I figured neither the good Lord nor the pope was going to make an issue out of it.)

When his classmates heard about what had happened, they were sad and afraid. Their grief and fear needed to be directed somewhere, so the school announced that the next evening there would be a prayer vigil for Ryland in our school chapel. Our chapel can accommodate about 250 people. It proved woefully inadequate. So many of our students and parents came that the overflow spilled out into the foyer and the hallways.

I had carefully planned a service centered on prayer and Scripture that would run about an hour. The folks there appreciated the structure, but they took it over and made it their own. One hour led to two, two hours led to three. It became obvious that the students needed to stand up and express their fears for Ryland, their anger at his choice, their hope for his recovery, and their pleas to watch out and care for each other. The parents told the young people, with tears in their eyes, how much they loved them. It was an extraordinary evening of prayer and support as well as a passionate affirmation of the value of each life.

All of us pledged that our prayers would not end there but would continue until Ryland recovered. Every Sunday throughout the long summer months, students and parents gathered in our quadrangle at precisely 2:00 P.M. to pray the rosary for Ryland and to be updated on his condition.

Ryland did recover, although not to the degree that we had prayed for. The damage to his spine confines him to a wheelchair. The damage to his brain makes it necessary for him to use a computer to communicate—a big improvement over the low-tech buzzer he used the first year, one buzz for "yes" and two for "no."

Ryland and I continued our conversations and friendship during his long hospitalization and his recovery in different care facilities. Although I asked him why he had wanted to end his life, he never told me. He never talked about the pain that had driven him to jump off that bridge. Maybe it was too difficult to revisit; maybe he simply didn't know why.

Only God knows why Ryland did what he did, but I was very pleased when one day he asked me to help him deal with the pain in his soul. Using his buzzer and pointing to letters in the alphabet with a stick in his mouth, he labored to tell me, "Father, I want to be baptized into the Catholic faith." I was delighted to begin a course of instruction and preparation with him. Because his attention span was short, I drew a series of amateurish cartoons. They were crude, but they did get across the central beliefs and practices of our faith. Ryland seemed to get a kick out of them. His frequent smiles alone made my efforts worthwhile. He was genuinely interested in the Christian faith, especially the Catholic expression of it with its emphasis on a personal God, human redemption, forgiveness, and grace. Its answers to life's mystery seemed to provide a healing and a hope for his damaged soul.

The day of his baptism Ryland sat proudly in his wheelchair, dressed in his finest. I wore with pride the shoes he had given me. They were my spiritual connection to Ryland's heart. I baptized him during one of the Sunday Masses in my parish of St. Matthew's. During the rite of baptism, the candidate answers a series of questions with the words, "I do." Although Ryland couldn't speak, you could clearly hear throughout the church the sound of the buzzer signaling his proud "I do!" to the series of questions. It was a great experience.

Baptism doesn't promise to take away the hurt and pain in a wounded soul. It won't cleanse people from the fog of depression and despair. That's the province of psychologists. But baptism lays a foundation for human life and the human journey. It defines our life and its purpose on this earth. Baptism proclaims that we are from God, that we find meaning for our life in a relationship with God, and that our life has a final destination, heaven.

Today, Ryland knows he's not alone in his struggles. God is with him, providing him with strength and a new vision of his life from his wheelchair.

CHAPTER THIRTY-TWO

Keeping the Flame Alive

Anthropologist Bruce Chatwin, in his book *Songlines*, relates a story that pops into my mind every time I hear someone talk about their fears that their life is running on empty, that the fire that fuels their ambitions and passions is dying.

On safari in Central Africa, Chatwin hired a dozen or so local people to carry his bulky equipment on their long trek. After traveling by foot for a number of days, suddenly and without explanation the locals untangled themselves from their burdens and sat down. They refused to go any further and seemed to have fallen into a trancelike state. No amount of bargaining could get them to budge. After three days, they got up, shouldered the equipment once again, and resumed the safari. Later, when Chatwin pressed them for an explanation, they explained, "We had gotten ahead of our spirit. We had to stay there until the spirit caught up with us."[11]

Such wisdom is as old as creation itself. In Genesis 2:1-3 we read that God's work of creation took six days and that on the seventh day he rested. Then God blessed the seventh day and made it holy. God went further and demanded that his people also observe a day of rest on the seventh day of the week (see Exodus 20:8-10). For the Jews, the seventh day of the week was the Sabbath Day, a word that literally means "to rest." God knew what he was doing.

We live increasingly stressful lives, trying to keep up with schedules and demands on our time and energy. No matter how much we do, more is demanded. No matter how much we accomplish, the next day awaits us with even more on our plates. At times the road ahead seems endless and the temptation to quit on the journey grows increasingly attractive. Some do simply drop out. Most fight through the temptation and continue on, but grow increasingly weary, afraid that fumes, not fuel, are powering them through the days and challenges of life. Their flame is flickering and they wonder how they can make it roar and come to life again.

Sometimes our bodies get way ahead of our spirits. Rather than push on, we would be wise to rest until our spirits have the chance to catch up with our bodies. Only when the two are reunited, working in tandem with each other, feeding off of each other, can we draw the strength we need to continue our journey. The spirit is home to our dreams, our passions, our hopes, our loves, our joys, the very meaning of our existence. If the body pushes ahead and leaves the spirit behind, disaster is inevitable. We will shut down and the flame will die. The fire will be extinguished.

Back in the 1970s, a very successful and very young head coach of a National Football League team led his team to the Super Bowl, the pinnacle of his profession. At the press conference after the game, he announced that he was resigning from coaching, effective immediately. The news stunned the reporters; they clamored for an explanation. Why would anyone who had made it to the top of his profession at such a young age turn his back on the big salary, fame, perks, and prestige and simply walk away? The coach's answer was, "I'm burned out!"

When people burn out, they no longer know why they are

doing what they are doing. "Why" is a spiritual question. It touches our soul, it fuels our ambitions, it drives our efforts, it keeps the flame alive. When we can't answer the "why" question, our efforts and energies lose any meaning beyond filling time or putting a roof over our heads and food on the table. When we get up in the morning we feel no joy.

When we, like the NFL coach, have no answer for why we do what we do, it's time to rest. To take a Sabbath.

That's what Jesus did. If anyone had cause to give up, he did. His life overflowed with stress and incredible demands. Thousands flocked to him as the one with the answer to their poverty, oppression, diseases, and fears. He knew firsthand the pain of rejection, false accusations, and threats by those who plotted his arrest and death. He knew the personal hurt of having his closest and most trusted friends turn their backs on him. His disciple Peter denied that he even knew him—not once but three times. Another betrayed him for thirty pieces of silver to the very ones who wanted him dead. His disciples often misunderstood his words, and at times didn't have a clue about the true nature of his mission.

Yet Jesus didn't quit, didn't drop out, didn't burn out. Why? He stopped, sat down, put aside his burden, and refused to move until his spirit caught up with his body. In the Gospels, we frequently find him withdrawing from the crowds and demands that pressed in on him. He would go off by himself or with a few of his disciples for a Sabbath time. It was then, through prayer and meditation, through fellowship with God the Father, that Jesus found the answer to the "why" question for himself. He got in touch with why God sent him into the world, why his mission would change the downward spiral of the human condition, why he had to suffer and die. This time enabled him to recommit himself to the necessary sacrifices and hardships that he would have to embrace to accomplish his work of the Kingdom of God. He came away from these Sabbath times refreshed, recommitted, renewed, the flame alive and burning brightly.

One such time occurred just hours away from his arrest (see Matthew 26:36-46). Knowing that his death was imminent, he asked his disciples to accompany him to the Garden of Gethsemane for prayer and time with the Father. At this vulnerable time, when Jesus needed the support of his friends, they promptly fell asleep, leaving him alone with his fears. At that moment Jesus wanted to quit, to flee what was ahead. "Father, if it is possible, let this cup pass from me," he prayed. But the temptation to quit didn't last long. Just seconds later, he added, "Not my will, but yours be done." His sense of purpose gave him strength.

Some might argue that burnout, depression, discouragement, stress, and anxiety are more properly handled by medication and the psychological sciences. Certainly these things have a place in the healing of a spent spirit and flickering flame. But the revival of our spirit must begin by connecting with the God who first created it with a divine purpose. It is God who ultimately holds the answer to the "why" of our lives.

I've taken frequent Sabbath times, ranging from a weeklong retreat to a few quick moments of prayer squeezed in at my most vulnerable times. Without such times of reconnecting with God, I would be a dentist somewhere in Seattle (my second career choice).

One of my most stressful times is Sunday at Mass just before

I go over to the pulpit to read the gospel and preach the day's sermon. Just before the priest enters the pulpit, our rubrics ask that we pray a little prayer that goes like this: "May the word of God be on my lips and in my heart so that I may worthily proclaim the gospel of the Lord." This wonderful centering prayer calls to mind what we are about to do. But it doesn't work for me. I look out at my brothers and sisters and read the hunger in their lives for the living God to speak to their needs. I know my own frailty and often think, *What am I doing here?*

So years ago, I changed the prayer to better express my feelings and needs. I bow my head and pray, "God, I'm not much, but I'm all you have right now. Use me for your purpose."

That tiny prayer calms my nerves, stills my temptation to flee, acknowledges the responsibility God has given me, seeks God's help, and reminds me of my purpose—to further God's kingdom. If I don't remember why I do what I do, my efforts to reach people with God's love is going to fall flat.

There was a time in American life when Sunday was truly a day of rest and renewal for most folks. There were no malls, stores by and large were closed for business, and the only people who worked were the ones whose jobs provided vital services such as police and fire protection. Sunday was observed as the Sabbath, a time for church services, Sunday picnics and family meals, a drive in the country, an afternoon in the park. Somehow we have allowed the demands of modern life to change Sunday into yet another day of stress, commerce, and anxiety. Church is squeezed in between time on the Internet and a hurried trip to the mall—if it isn't skipped entirely because it's just another workday. And we are paying a terrible price.

But even though the Sabbath has been abandoned by others, you and I can still take Sabbath rests. We can take the time to let our spirits catch up with our bodies. We can take time to get in touch with the "why" of our lives. If we do, we'll keep the flame alive.

CONCLUSION

When I left home for the seminary to study to become a priest, my younger sister always told her friends that I was in the cemetery. The two words do sound alike, and I'm sure some people think the excitement level is the same in both places. But for me, seminary was a source of spiritual adrenaline as I anticipated my lifework of bringing hope to a broken world and light to lead people out of darkness.

In 1968, sixteen of us in all were ordained priests for the Archdiocese of Seattle, a territory comprising all of Western Washington. At ordination, we were eager to start our ministry, convinced of the critical importance of our work, and secure in the knowledge that God would provide for all of our needs.

Twenty-five years later, in 1993, the *Seattle Times* newspaper assigned a reporter to do a feature story on the sixteen of us and what had happened in our lives since our ordination. "Where Are All the Priests?" attempted to put a human face on the numerous studies and research done on the declining number of priests in America.

My ordination class proved typical of the trends and numbers across the country. Of the sixteen of us ordained, only six are still priests. Each of us has a different reason for why we remained priests, but it really comes down to one word: joy.

Joy is a deeply, deeply spiritual gift. When one receives it, life becomes so securely anchored that no storm can overwhelm or sweep us away. Joy is the capacity to experience delight and bliss in life, in our relationships and in our work. Joy comes from God as a gift when we enter into a relationship with him. St. Paul teaches that one of the fruits produced in a life connected to God's Spirit is joy (see Galatians 5:22).

We find joy when we discover that our life is a critically important thread in the hands of God, who weaves it with other lives into a beautiful tapestry. He is crafting what Christians call the Kingdom of God. Secure in this knowledge, we can be joyful in good times and bad, in moments of defeat as well as success. Joy brings meaning, wonder, and motivation to the most mundane tasks and experiences. Nothing can rob us of it when we are bound to God.

A reporter for a local newspaper was assigned to do a feature story on the town's major industry, a nearby stone quarry. With notepad and pen, he began his research by going to the quarry and interviewing the stonecutters employed there. Seeking a special angle for his story, he asked one of the workers, "What does your work mean to you?" A very unhappy man, the stonecutter replied in a surly voice, "I cut stone all day for one reason. I need the money it brings to live." With that, he went back to his work and the reporter moved on to a second worker and asked the same question.

This man replied with a somewhat more noble response: "I cut stone so that I can provide a life for my wife and children and fulfill my responsibilities as a husband and father."

Finally, the reporter moved on to a third worker and asked again, "What does your work mean to you?" The question animated the stonecutter, and he came alive with a sparkle in his eyes and a melody in his voice. "I'm cutting the stone that will build a great cathedral, a place that will honor God and serve as the sacred space where our children and their children's children will come to know the loving God for centuries to come. This is the work that God has given me. That's what my work means to me."[12]

All three stonecutters performed the same task, held the same job. Yet each of them saw their work in a vastly different light, with a significantly different purpose. The first worker couldn't see beyond himself and what his labor would bring to him immediately and materially. He was a very unhappy man and took no satisfaction in his work. The second stonecutter had a nobler and less self-serving view of his work. He took satisfaction in knowing that his labor provided for the needs of his family. He was a happy man. The third stonecutter saw his work as tied to the most noble and honorable task of all, serving God and his people, bringing them together, furthering God's plan. He was a joyful man!

Material things can bring us happiness, but all of us hunger for more. We want joy—and that can't be found on the shelves of our department stores or in the showrooms of our automobile dealers. Joy is God's gift. One of my favorite and most centering verses in Scripture is contained in a psalm of praise called the "Magnificat," uttered by Mary when she was pregnant with Jesus during her visit to her cousin Elizabeth. Ecstatic that God has chosen her to bring the Savior into the world, Mary prays, "My spirit rejoices in God my savior" (Luke 1:47). With those beautiful words, Mary points out that joy comes to the human soul when we surrender to God and allow him to use our life in his plan for human redemption and the building of his kingdom.

One doesn't have to be a priest to possess joy. I've known priests who were joyless, unhappy, and disgruntled in their work and calling. I've known sanitation workers who were joyful and fulfilled in their work. Joy comes to those who see their life being used by God.

I've found a great deal of joy in my work as a priest. Priests are invited into people's lives at their weakest and lowest moments, and we're asked to be strong for them. We are invited to be present and celebrate their marriages, the baptisms of their children, the funerals of their loved ones. Daily we work alongside others in building a community of faith, a cathedral of people, where together we are formed and nourished by the Word and by the presence of the living God.

I remember a commercial that aired many years ago. It began with a beautiful picture of the universe, a black background with millions of twinkling stars. The announcer then began to ask questions of profound significance. "What is the meaning of our lives? Are they purposeful or random? Why are we here? Is there intelligence behind our existence?" The picture of the universe then fades and is replaced by a picture of the product, which I don't remember. The announcer comes back on and says, "(Our product.) It may not be the answer, but at least it's not another question!"

I have found joy in my work not because I am a priest but because my Christian faith holds the answers to the questions raised in that old commercial. As a priest, every time someone approaches me and says, "Hey, Father!" I get to open the door to God's teachings and truth. I can't think of anything else I'd rather do.